AN ACCIDENTAL MURDER

and

Other Stories

AN ACCIDENTAL MURDER

and

Other Stories

Diana M. Grillo

An Accidental Murder and Other Stories
Copyright © 2018 by Diana M. Grillo

This is a work of fiction. Names, characters, businesses, places, events, locales, and incidents are either the products of the author's imagination or used in a fictitious manner. Any resemblance to actual persons, living or dead, or actual events is purely coincidental.

"Mr. Anderson" was first published in *Boundless*, a short story collection, Vinculinc Anthology, and its website, vinculinc.com

Cover Art by Dan Long, Abstract Expressionist Artist, Scottsdale, Arizona http://arizonafineartexpo.com/daniel-long/

ISBN 978-1-7321315-0-7

Printed in USA

For Laura

This book is dedicated to the loving memory of my beautiful and talented daughter, Laura. She took me on a journey in life that I could never have imagined. She was not only my daughter but also my best friend. Her smile, her laugh and her love of life lives on in her daughter, Tess. Love and miss you, Laura. Mom.

TABLE OF CONTENTS

Foreword

While it is not customary for an editor to write a foreword for a writer's first collection of short stories, I gladly accepted Diana's request for my comments on the collection from a different point of view—as a friend and fellow writer. Diana and I knew each other as young children in the same neighborhood, and developed a friendship working on a school reunion many years later. As I read her deceptively simple stories, I became increasingly impressed with how much lay beneath the surface.

Diana Grillo is, by her definition, a new writer, having taken up her pen almost as therapy a few years ago after a period of grief over the loss of her beloved daughter. She draws from her own experiences and observations as a child growing up poor in a wealthy neighborhood, as a young single mother working her way through school, and as an adult working in the legal profession.

The stories in *An Accidental Murder* capture in spare prose and telling detail the everyday experiences of children and adults, mainly women, who live with the constant threat of one kind of abuse or another. These stories were written (and the collection conceived) long before the themes of abuse, violence, harassment and poverty became news headlines and the subjects of TV series. Diana's characters are not famous or glamorous. They are people who were born into their circumstances, and in most cases hadn't learned early enough how to make the best choices for themselves. The events are not singular dramatic events of the kind making headlines, but part of the daily fabric of their lives.

The children in "Betrayal" and "The Closet" endure thoughtless cruelty and parental neglect that threatens their health and well-being. "The Trip" and "Mr. Anderson" both feature a young girl whose landscape is a minefield of unprovoked anger ready to explode no matter which direction she steps. In "Comeuppance," a woman can't leave a cheating husband even though he treats her with open disdain and disrespect.

Life is not all bleak for these characters. There are best friends to play and grow up with; older brothers to teach and protect them; other adults—neighbors, friends' families, coworkers—to help them find love and kindness, beauty and truth, justice and hope in their worlds. Although the characters vary in personality and place in life, a thread of continuity runs through the stories; they feel connected.

An Accidental Murder is a book of stories about suffering, yes, but also about the ways an individual finds to escape or overcome or seek justice in one way or another. And while we might consider these characters "victims" of abuse, neglect, violence, poverty and many other indignities, most of Diana Grillo's characters never succumb to the passivity of victimhood. They don't end up as victims. They have, or they gain, agency.

Many of the young characters in these stories make use of one of the few tools a child in these circumstances has to cope—constant vigilance, like prisoners waiting for a chance to escape. The little girl in "Betrayal" is keenly observant, always watching and listening to the adults around her, finding a kind of guidance in their behavior patterns and rituals. She seeks comfort in the arms of a prized stuffed koala bear—even if only in her imagination. In "The Closet," a pre-teen puts her faith in her older brother to protect them from the wrath of their father. The teenager in "The Trip" summons up the courage to take charge on the walk home in the dark with the teen boy who she just met on a blind date. A single mom, waitressing to make ends meet, finds the goodness in each of the cast of crazy characters she works with at "The Steak & Brew." In both "The Apartment" and "The Little Black Box" a woman puts up with the destructive and selfish behavior of a husband for just so long.

While sharing themes and circumstances with others, the title story, "An Accidental Murder," is a kind of aberration among the eleven. But in context, it takes on greater meaning. Perhaps we see a young woman's wish or fear or hope that those who abuse will get their comeuppance. In a later story, called "Comeuppance," they do.

The effect of the stories is cumulative. Although each story is self-contained, each one raises echoes of previous stories, and in the end makes the experience of reading the collection much more than the sum of its eleven stories.

After reading all of them, your feeling about the small abused and neglected girl in an earlier story may evolve, and you realize that she grew up and found her way as an adult into a bigger world where she could thrive.

Ginger E. Benlifer, a mutual friend who is an avid reader and a psychologist, summed up the collection perfectly using an image from one of the stories:

"The tear examined under a microscope aptly describes the totality of this very special collection."

Lauren O'Neill
Freelance Writer and Editor

BETRAYAL

THE THICK, WOOL koala bear with small, outstretched arms, gray ears and black dots for eyes and a nose, stared at me from the window of Anderson's bookstore. He was perched atop a pile of books. I couldn't help myself from stopping to say "hi" to him every time I passed the store. I wanted to take him home, hug him and take him to bed with me. I was sure he would be much happier with me than sitting in that dusty bookstore staring out the window. As Koala looked back at me from the window, I was suddenly torn away. My mother grabbed my hand and pulled me along. "Maria, hurry up, stop daydreaming," she said. "We have to get to the doctor's office, I'm not feeling well."

The year was 1955. I was eight years old, a skinny little girl with a protruding nose that hadn't caught up with her face yet. Most of my memories of Dr. Russo were of the times he made house calls to our apartment, but this day was different. This was the day I found out my mother never really wanted me.

My mother and Dr. Russo met years ago, when she was a young mother escaping the pollution of New York

City. My older brother was a sickly child and the doctors advised her to move to the clean air of suburban Westchester County. Since my mother was Italian, and spoke Italian, she, of course, tried to find an Italian doctor. Dr. Russo was the only Italian doctor in Larchmont, a rare find, since we lived in what at the time was the Waspiest town in Westchester.

I'll never forget Dr. Russo's house calls. I was the youngest of three children; there was always someone who was sick and in need of a house call. For my mother, Dr. Russo's calls were like a visit from an old friend. She would offer him "coffee and—." The "and" was whatever treat, cake or cookie was available. Dr. Russo was always too busy for "coffee and—," so he always said, "No, thank you, I have a lot of people to see today." But he was never too busy to carefully examine his first patient, the Playboy Calendar hanging on our living room wall.

The annual Playboy Calendar was my father's idea of art. It hung on a small nail, so that when January was over, Miss January wearing her New Year's hat and not much else could be lifted up and placed on the nail above to make room for Miss February. Dr. Russo would slowly examine each month's playgirl. Occasionally I watched him but most often I was lying in the bedroom waiting. I could hear his diagnosis: "Well, now Miss December is really beautiful."

When I looked up at my mother after she pulled me away from Koala, I saw that her mouth was twitching. I could feel her hands shaking as we walked on to Dr. Russo's office. My parents never quite adjusted to living in the suburbs, so despite the fact that a car was a necessity, they never learned to drive and never owned a car. We walked everywhere.

Dr. Russo's office was in the basement of his home. He had recently torn down his old house and built a new one. There were rumors that the neighbors weren't happy about his modern looking house with large glass windows and slanted roofs. It rose high above the more traditional houses with their wraparound porches. Dr. Russo was well respected and liked in the community, but that was not true of his wife. She was in constant fights with her neighbors and some believed she built this modern style house just to spite her many enemies.

As we walked down the steps and into Dr. Russo's office I could see the crowded waiting room. We may have lived in the Waspiest of towns, but visiting Dr. Russo's office was like stepping into Little Italy. The waiting room was large; chairs filled with patients were lined up against the walls. There were mostly older looking men in scruffy work clothes with worn-out hats on their heads. Their hands were thick with calluses and gritty from work. There were several women wearing black dresses and thick black shoes and a few young children playing on the floor. Mother and I found a seat and waited like everyone else. I watched as my mother's shaking hand opened her purse and reached in. I could hear the pill bottles rattling around at the bottom of her purse. She had pulled out a tissue and had begun wiping her eyes, when she recognized an older woman sitting across from us. She got up and went over to the women. They kissed and began speaking rapidly in Italian. I remember looking around at all the people, trying to figure out what was wrong with them. They were all speaking Italian and I couldn't understand what they were saying. My mother and father spoke Italian in our home like it was a code, only to be used when they didn't want anyone to know what they were saying. Occasionally, someone would shift from Italian to English. Then I was all ears.

Every once in a while, Dr. Russo would open the exam room door and say "next," and someone would follow him inside. Eventually the faces in the waiting room would change, people would visit the doctor and leave, and more people would come in. Finally, my mother took my hand and said it was our turn.

I don't remember what was wrong with my mother or why we were there on this day. But I do know that the story of what happened next was repeated over and over for many years to come.

Dr. Russo was a plump short man with a kind face. He greeted us that day by saying, "Hi Connie, what's the matter now?" He then turned to me and said, "Look how beautiful she is—didn't I tell you not to get rid of her."

"You lied to me," my mother said. "You knew I didn't want to have another baby and you told me those pills would take care of it, but they didn't."

Looking down at me Dr. Russo said matter-of-factly, "Well aren't you glad now? Look how beautiful she is." My mother gave him that look, the look that said, I guess so. It wasn't hard for me to figure out that my mother had not wanted me and had tried to get rid of me.

Dr. Russo examined my mother and after a while he told her, "It's your nerves, Connie. You're too nervous. You have to calm down." He gently stroked her face and patted it a few times. "I'll give you some more nerve pills. Are you taking the ones I gave you the last time?" My mother nodded yes. "You'll be fine," he told her. "Just keep taking the nerve pills." He smiled. "OK, that will be five dollars." As soon as he said that I could see the look of panic on my mother's face.

While my mother stood twitching nervously, I sat on the examination table. It had become my seat of choice over the years as I watched what I named the "Five-Dollar Ballet." The five-dollar ballet would repeat over and over, almost action-for-action, word-for-word. "Five dollars!" my mother said. "I can't give you five dollars. It's all Joseph gives me for the week, you know I have two other kids at home."

Dr. Russo replied with stern conviction, "Well, five dollars is my office fee."

My mother began her search for the five-dollar bill. Her hand shook as she reached into her large purse; the rattling sound of her nerve pills went on until she slowly, painfully pulled the five-dollar bill out of her wallet and held it out.

Thus began the tug of war. My mother faced Dr. Russo while she kept a tight grip on one end of the five-dollar bill and Dr. Russo grabbed onto the other end to take it. I watched as the five-dollar bill moved like a ballet in midair from one side to the other. One moment it slid close to my mother, then back to Dr. Russo. I moved my head from side to side, watching the bill as they tugged it back and forth, wondering if it would eventually rip in two. All the while, Dr. Russo and my mother kept up the dialogue.

"Dr. Russo, Joseph only gives me five dollars for the week and I have to make that last. You know what he's like, he won't give me any more." She took a step closer to Dr. Russo. "I have to buy everything I need with that five dollars. I just can't give you all of it."

Dr. Russo, exasperated, said, "Connie, I know but it's my fee."

He turned to me as though I could help him. I stared at him and said nothing. I had the feeling he was telling me, hey I saved your life, can't you help me. I couldn't help wishing that I had that five-dollar bill, so I could run back to Anderson's and buy my Koala.

Dr. Russo pushed his glasses up closer to his nose in frustration. "I have to charge you my fee; I can't do this for nothing."

I watched closely to see if my mother would say OK, take the five dollars, but that never happened. "I know, I know, but I can't give you all of it, I'll have nothing for the rest of the week." She was pleading.

The ballet of the five-dollar bill went on, the bill dancing back and forth until finally, Dr. Russo gave me a look of defeat and said to my mother, "OK, give me the bill and I'll give you some change."

At that moment, the bill slipped from my mother's hands into Dr. Russo's. He opened his desk drawer and set the five-dollar bill into a box. He pulled out a few ones, gave them to my mother, and the ballet was over.

CLOSET DOOR

WE LIVED IN a small one-bedroom apartment, five people. I assume when all three of us kids were young, the apartment didn't appear as small to us, but we were growing up now and bumping into each other. My father was too cheap to get a larger apartment, so there we stayed.

Our bedroom had two windows that faced the New Haven railroad tracks, a short trip to New York City. Between us and the tracks was a parking lot for commuters, and above the parking lot, a rock cliff wall. One night we heard a loud noise, which we later found out was a gunshot. That was the only shooting I remember taking place in our quiet and safe town. A man had been robbing the bowling alley across the street, and a cop chased him and shot him. I'm not sure if the cop killed him, or the fall did, but in any case, he dropped off the rock cliff onto the parking lot. I can still see the white chalk outline of his body.

The most interesting feature of our bedroom was the huge closet door at the far end of the room that was full of holes. My brother had decided to take out his anger at my father by throwing knives at the door. He did this so often that the door resembled a carnival knife-throwing board. I used to imagine a beautiful woman with flowing blond hair standing in front of the door as my brother threw his knife at her. I would yell, "Get out of the way, lady, he doesn't know what he's doing."

I knew there was another reason he destroyed the door. He had a recurring dream, a nightmare in which he was dragged into the closet and chased by monsters. He would tell me his monster dreams in such vivid detail that I remember them as though I dreamt them myself. They became my dreams.

One day, as I sat on the edge of the bed crying, I looked up at my brother. He was bent over his microscope. He said, "What are you crying about?"

"He won't let me see *The Wizard of Oz*. I really want to see it!"

He just gave me that look. *You know what he's like, so why cry about it?* I knew he was right; my father would never let me see the movie. Crying was not going to do me any good. But I just wanted to cry.

"Oh, stop crying. Come over here and give me one of your tears," my brother said.

"Why should I? What for?" I said.

"So I can look at it under the microscope."

Before I could say anything, I felt the cold hard piece of glass under my eye, capturing my tear. I watched my brother as he carefully slid it under the microscope and adjusted it to see the tear more clearly. I said," I want to see. It's my tear."

"Well come and see it then. And stop crying."

I studied my tear through the microscope, and before

long I forgot about how sad I was. I'll never forget that night.

My brother was just two years older than me, so we played together often. We blasted off into space in our cardboard box spaceship; we fought the cowboy and Indian wars with his miniature figures. When he was frustrated with me, he would put the palm of his hand on my forehead, pushing me back a little, and tell me, "You were supposed to be a boy." I knew he really wanted a younger brother, so I tried to do boy things to make him happy.

I was his little sister and playmate, and later, as we got older, he also made me his exercise partner. My brother would lie on the living room floor and yell to me, "Come over here and hold my feet down." I'd bend down on the floor and grab hold of his ankles while he did his sit ups. Then he would hoist me up on his knees and use me as a weight while he bent down and did his squats. He was always exercising. I knew he was building himself up so that one day he could protect himself from my father. I looked forward to seeing my brother get even with my father, and I wanted that day to come soon.

That day came, but it was a long time after the night he put my tear under the microscope. We were teenagers, now living in a rental that was part of a single-family home cut up into apartments.

It was early June, hot and muggy outside. My hair was wet with sweat as I walked home from school that day. Inside, I saw my mother sitting on the sofa with my father next to her; he looked pale and sickly. I knew he had a heart condition, but he wasn't just sick. I could tell this was different.

"What's the matter, what happened?" I said.

My mother said, "Your brother almost killed your father."

With interest and hidden indifference, I asked, "What'd he do?"

"He punched him, and I found him on the floor. He's a very sick man you know," my mother said as she tended to my father. "Go and look in the kitchen and see what your brother did."

When I walked into the kitchen, I saw what looked like a pile of metal on the floor. It resembled a crime scene, jagged metal scattered in all directions. When I moved closer I could see that it had once been our food cabinet. A few crushed cans of green beans had rolled across the floor. There was a squashed box of pasta pushed into the corner of what was once a metal shelf. In a normal home, there may have been shelves full of canned goods, cereal, snacks, coffee in the cabinet, but in our house, it was just a metal cabinet with a door. The most I ever remember seeing in it were the few cans of green beans and boxes of pasta that were now laying on the floor. Sometimes I'd open the door and just stare at the empty shelves, thinking it would be nice to see shelves filled with food in there. At times, I would even talk to the empty shelves: "You really want to be full of food, don't you?" Now that it was gone, it made me a little sad.

We never had enough food in the house. It may not have mattered so much when we were young and didn't eat very much, but as we grew up, we needed more food. Unfortunately, the twenty-dollar food budget my father allowed didn't grow up with us. It stayed the same. Our being hungry and needing more food were not reasons for my father to spend any more money. He controlled the food budget, so when the food was gone, there was no more, need or not.

My brother had stopped talking to my father long ago. We both spent as little time at home as possible. We stayed with friends or left the house sometimes just to get enough to eat.

When my brother finally came home that night, I cornered him to get all the details about what happened. That day I had waited for, had come, and I missed it. I felt robbed. I had helped him get into shape for this, and I wanted a front row seat. It just wasn't fair.

I said, "I can't believe you did it. Tell me all about it."

He said, "What do you want to know that for? Just forget about it."

I said, "No, I want to know everything. Tell me."

As he began to talk, I put myself in the kitchen in the front row seat. And, just as I did when we were kids and he told me about the monsters in the closet, I was there, watching everything that happened.

When he came home from school, and saw my father in the living room, he ignored him as always. He was starving so he went into the kitchen to look for something to eat, but there was nothing. By the time he got to the tall metal cabinet, he was not only hungry, but really pissed off. If this cabinet were alive, it would have braced itself for what was about to happen. He opened and closed the cabinet door, and then stepped back from it. No food. He had this look on his face, a look that said, "I have got to find food." He opened the cabinet door again, and then slammed it so hard it shut and swung open again. It was like it was telling him, "go ahead, do it again." He kept opening and slamming the door as hard as he could until finally, the defiant door hung there, defeated. Then he began to assault the top. He made a fist and lifted his arm up high and slammed it down, pounding on the cabinet with no mercy, yelling, "FOOD. I NEED FOOD." He kept hitting the cabinet, blow after blow, and with each pound of his fist, it bent and twisted and flattened. He kept hitting it — FOOD! FOOD! FOOD! — until it looked like a crumpled accordion. Now it was just a pile of scrap metal on the floor.

I wondered, if the cabinet had had any food in it, as it should have, would he have been able to squash it like a bug? But then I remembered how he had changed from the skinny, sickly kid he was. He was strong now with muscles in his arms. I couldn't help feeling a little proud of his muscles, since I had been, willing or not, his constant exercise assistant.

The story wasn't over. I said, "Wow! I saw the cabinet. Or what's left of it. You demolished it." His next words brought me back into the kitchen with him.

He was still finishing off the cabinet when my father came into the kitchen. He sneaked up behind my brother, grabbed a dinner plate, lifted it up with both hands and hit him over the head. The plate shattered and fell to the ground.

If I really had been there I would have yelled, "Turn around, turn around! He's behind you and he's going to hit you."

My brother's body bent down at the waist from the

force of the blow. He was hurt; his hands reflexively grabbed his head. Within a split second he made a fist, and spun around towards my father, with a fierce look in his eyes. He cocked his fists, and just as every fighter in a title fight dreams of doing, he landed a knockout punch.

My father went down hard.

"Wow! You really did it." I just looked at my brother.

"I didn't know what happened at first," he said. "He hit me from behind, and all I knew was that it hurt so much, I turned around and punched the evil bastard. He fell, and I left." My brother looked up at me. "Is he still alive?"

I said, "Yes, they had the doctor here. I guess he's OK."

Wow! I thought. One punch was all it took. Finally, he got what was coming to him, and no one deserved it more than him.

Not long afterward the scrap metal was taken out of the kitchen. We never did get another food cabinet. No need for it. One thing did change: my father never hit my brother again.

THE TRIP

IT WAS THE summer of 1964. The hit movie was Bye Bye Birdie, and I was turning sixteen at the end of July. My friend Julie had invited me to Fire Island for two weeks. My old blue suitcase sat hidden high up on the closet shelf. When I reached up to pull it down the night before I was to leave, it hit me on the side of my head. Damn! This was not a good start. Then, when I opened the suitcase, I had to back away from the strong musty smell. Now I'd have to leave it open all night and hope it would air out. I wished I had a new fresh-smelling suitcase with a silky, patterned material lining inside, but that was just a wish. I was eager to go on this trip and wanted to be ready, so I carefully folded my clothes and laid them out next to the suitcase. I'd pack in the morning. Much later that evening I heard them arguing.

"Don't think I'm giving her one red cent to go on this trip," my father yelled at my mother while he paced the living room floor.

"She doesn't need any money. They invited her, and Ruthie's paying for everything," my mother said, pleading for me to go.

The summer heat that morning was already sweltering, making me sweat as I packed as quickly as I could. Julie's mother, Ruthie, was picking me up in a taxi in a half hour. Whenever I could leave my house and get away from him was a good time.

Julie was more like a sister to me than a friend. We grew up in the same apartment building. When we were young we played together all the time; we played with dolls and ran into the woods playing tag. We'd sit for hours in her bedroom playing with her toys. Her favorite was a stuffed animal named Wolfie. We played with him until he was so worn out that he no longer resembled a wolf. His eyes were hanging off, and his dark brown fur was frayed, and he had bald spots. I loved Wolfie like he was my own.

Now we were teenagers, and Wolfie was tucked away in a closet. Julie and I double dated and went to parties, parades and the Fireman's carnival together. Told lies for each other to keep out of trouble. We thought about boys, talked about boys, and looked for boys. We were boy crazy.

As soon as I saw the taxi pull up, I grabbed my suitcase and ran out. We had a long trip to Bay Shore before we got to the ferry to take us to Fire Island. But just sitting in the taxi with Ruthie made me feel like I was on vacation already.

Ruthie was a nurse. Her favorite saying was, "Life stinks, and all men are B's." She kept a framed photo of herself as a young nurse displayed on top of a wooden chest in her living room. In the photo, she's dressed in her white nursing uniform, with a small stiff-looking nursing cap resting on top of her hair. I always thought the hat looked like a bird's nest sitting on a flimsy tree branch. The photo reminded me of those recruiting posters for WW II nurses: "Serve Your Country and Become an Army Nurse. Sign Up Today." Ruthie was never an Army nurse. She worked at our local hospital. If you asked Ruthie a nursing question in front of Julie, Julie would say, "Don't ask her, she doesn't know anything about nursing."

As soon as we were settled into our seats on the train, Ruthie reached into her purse and pulled out her lipstick. Here goes the lipstick routine, I thought. Ruthie had this habit of constantly putting on lipstick. She would carefully roll it up as far as it would go—it was always blood red. With her mirror in one hand and lipstick in the other, she'd smear it all over her lips, then press both lips tight together several times. This time, some red got on her tooth; she saw it and used her pinky finger to rub it off. Then she smiled at herself in the mirror. She was happy; her lips were bright red again. Watching her now I wanted to scream. You don't need any more lipstick; you have too much on already. But I didn't say anything; I just watched.

On the ferry, I stood close to the railing and leaned over so I could smell the salt air and watch the waves as we moved across the water. Seagulls circled the boat as though they were welcoming me to the island. Our ferry stop was Ocean Beach, known for the beautiful white lighthouse that towers above the town. As the ferry drew closer to shore, I could see Julie waving to us, her blond hair blowing in the wind. She was in her bathing suit and stood in her bare feet, holding the handle of a little red wagon. Red wagons are the cars of the island, the only way you can get anything from town to your home.

When we reached Julie, Ruthie gave her a big kiss and said, "How is my BD?" (BD meaning "beautiful daughter.") Julie kissed her back with an embarrassed look on her face. I was sure Ruthie was going to take out her lipstick and put some on right there, but she didn't. Ruthie loved Julie. But it was a love that had strings attached, and that included doing as much for Ruthie as Julie could stand.

The walk to the house was a winding, sandy pathway. We passed lush island greenery and beautiful flowers. Every house on Fire Island has a name like "Beach Bum" or "Little Hideaway." When we reached their place, Julie's grandparents came outside to meet us. Her father trailed behind, looking very thin and frail. The family greeted us warmly with hugs and kisses. I noticed that Ruthie seemed to shrink into a child as soon as she saw her parents. They held her tight and called her Ruthie dear. She was their only child.

Julie's grandfather had been a Merchant Marine. He built the house on Fire Island to resemble a ship and decorated it with nautical items. There was a built-in table with benches in the kitchen, which looked like a ship's galley. Pictures of the ocean and boats lined the living room walls. There were doilies on the furniture and a beautiful piano in the back of the room. The house had several bedrooms. My room was a small area with just a bed. Curtains decorated with blue sailboats hung in the place of a door that I could pull closed for privacy. I loved it.

Julie's father had just been diagnosed with cancer, and the family was told he had only a few more months to live. He had quit working immediately. Now, he was spending as much time with Julie, Ruthie and his family as he could. He loved to fish, so he stayed on Fire Island fishing and enjoying the ocean. I knew he was sick, and it made me so sad. I had known him for years, but I never truly knew him until that summer.

Julie and I sat around the house talking and doing our nails. We walked all over the island, took bike trips and lay on the beach. There was a boy that Julie liked, and had started seeing before I arrived. She said he had a friend and they wanted to meet up with us that night. The meeting place was an abandoned car that was hidden somewhere not far from the shore.

"How did a car get on the island?" I asked.

"I don't know, but he said it was there. Come on, let's go."

Julie started to walk off the path. "Julie, there's no path here. Where are we going?"

"Don't worry. It's OK. I know the way."

We walked for a long time through the thick brush and sandy area. We'd left before dark, but it was pitch black when we finally reached the car sitting in the patch of sand and brush. How strange, I thought. The boys were standing by the car when we got there. Julie introduced everyone.

It wasn't long before Julie was in the back seat with her boyfriend, making out. I sat in the front seat with the other guy. He was tall and heavyset, and I don't remember his real name because in my mind I had named him the "Big Galoop, "which I later shortened to "The BG." We were talking about movies and he asked me if I had seen Bye Bye Birdie yet. I barely had a chance to say no, when he leaned in and turned my face to his and tried to kiss me. I pushed him away and said, "No! Stop it." He moved away, and we sat and talked some more. He told me he lived in the same town as I did and said when I got back home I should call him. He wrote his phone number on a piece of paper and handed it to me; I stuck it in my purse. I had just laughed at some joke he told when I noticed him sliding closer to me. Then he put his arm around me and tried to kiss me again.

"Stop doing that!" I said. "I have a boyfriend at home (I lied) and I don't cheat on him."

I looked back at Julie. "Julie. Let's go, it's getting late."

Julie said, "OK, in a little while."

"If you have a boyfriend what are you doing here?" The BG asked.

"Julie wanted to see Jerry."

"Well, you're here with me now, and your so-called boyfriend isn't here, so why can't we just have a good time together."

"But I'm not having a good time."

I looked back at Julie. "I'm leaving now."

"No, don't leave yet. We'll leave together—soon."

I knew Julie wasn't going anywhere. It was so dark out, I was scared to walk alone and I was sure I would get lost. I had no choice but to ask The BG to take me back.

"Can you help me get back to the path so I can go home?"

"No, don't go." He was almost pleading. I grabbed the door handle.

"I don't know where I am. Will you please help me get back?"

"All right … I'll take you back," he said in a defeated voice.

When we got out of the car, I could see how big he was. He towered over me. He reminded me of our school football players. Suddenly I was scared of him. I had this vision in my head that he would attack me and kill me on the way back. I'd be lying in the sand dead, and Julie would find me. She would scream, "Maggie, what have I done? It's all my fault, just because I wanted to meet my boyfriend." There'd be a manhunt for The BG. The police with their sniffing dogs would be combing the beach in search of him.

As we started to walk, I could feel sweat running down my face. What are you doing? Get hold of yourself and just get back home alive.

"You walk on that side of the brush, and I'll walk on this side," I told The BG.

He moved over to the other side as I had told him to. I felt better with him not so close to me. I kept an eye on him to make sure he stayed on his side.

"I'm a nice guy," he said. "You have nothing to be scared of."

"I'm not scared of you." (I lied again.) "I just wanted to leave. So, just stay on your side and keep walking." When we reached the path, and I could find my way, we parted. But I only felt safe when I entered the house. I sat on my bed, pulled the sailboat curtain shut and thought about how crazy I'd acted. Maybe he was just a nice guy who just wanted to kiss me.

When Julie finally got home, I told her I was mad at her for not leaving with me, but that didn't last long. She plopped on my bed and started telling me how much she liked this Jerry and how she loved kissing him. We talked for a long time. I could never stay mad at Julie.

I woke up early the next day and remembered it was my birthday; I was now officially sixteen. I could hear noises in the living room; everyone was up already. When I came out, Julie and her family gathered around me, all wishing me a happy birthday. They had arranged an early morning party, complete with cake, just for me. There were lots of cards and gifts on the wooden coffee table. Julie's father handed me the gift he had made for me. It was a beautiful photo frame decorated with brightly colored flowers and birds, and a handmade birthday card. It was so sweet; I was touched that he had put so much care into making a present for me. I felt happy and sad at the same time. I knew how sick he was and that he wouldn't be here for my next birthday.

When I arrived home, I was still thinking about Fire Island and the fun I had with Julie and her family. I pulled my suitcase and bag of gifts out of the taxi and up to the front door. Hearing voices in the backyard, I decided to walk to the back to see who was there. The grass was wet and had that just-rained fragrance. Once I recognized the voices of my father and his brother, my uncle Dominick, I quickly turned around to go back to the front door, but my uncle saw me.

"Hi, Maggie! Come over here. I haven't seen you in years." Now I had to walk over to them.

My uncle had features similar to my father's, but he was a much younger man. He was a kind person, at least what I knew of him. That was the big difference between them.

"I heard you were away…did you have a good time?"

"Yes, I did. I was on Fire Island with my friend Julie and her family."

"Oh, how nice."

I knew this could be trouble for me. As my uncle kept talking to me, I could see my father getting angry. I was taking his time away from his brother. Each time I tried to end the conversation and go into the house my uncle would ask another question. I knew if I didn't answer his questions, or my father thought I was rude to him, I would be in trouble and get hit. But if I spent too much time with him, I would still be in trouble and get hit.

I had put the suitcase down but was still holding the bag full of the gifts. I noticed that Uncle Dominick was peering into it. I told him about the trip and the surprise birthday party, with the cake and gifts and all. He wanted to see the gifts, so I showed them to him.

"So, you just had a birthday. How old are you now?"

"I'm sixteen."

He reached into his pocket and took out his wallet; he pulled out a five-dollar bill.

"Here. Take this. For your birthday."

"No, it's OK, I'm fine."

"Don't be silly, take it. It's a birthday gift."

I smiled, took the five dollars and thanked my uncle. I could see my father watching, and I feared what he was thinking. As soon as I could get away, I went into the house.

After my uncle had left, my father came into my bedroom and pulled me close to him.

"Why did you do that?" He yelled in my face.

"Do what?"

"You know what. You deliberately told my brother you had a birthday so he would give you that money."

"No, I didn't. He kept asking me questions—I was just answering them."

I could see the rage on my father's face; I turned to get away from him, but he came closer. He grabbed me, squeezing my arm tight then drew his hand back and slapped me across the face hard. And then he hit me again.

He yelled, "Don't ever do that again."

As soon as he let go of me, I backed up to get away from him. He left the room. He was finished.

I put my suitcase on the bed to unpack and tried to forget what had just happened. My face was red hot and stinging; I rubbed my cheek. The heat and the redness would subside. The pain would take a lot longer.

As I was taking my things out of the suitcase, the frame and handmade card from Julie's father fell to the floor. I picked them up carefully, making sure not to disturb the flowers. I stared at them for a long time. A teardrop fell on the frame. I quickly wiped it off; it was much too beautiful to have a tearstain on it.

Later that night, I put the frame and my clothes back into my suitcase. I dug out the paper with The BG's phone number from the bottom of my purse and stuffed it in my wallet next to the five-dollar bill. I picked up my purse and suitcase and went outside. The sky was dark, almost pitch black, reminding me of that night on Fire Island. I started walking.

THE APARTMENT

OH NO, IT'S starting again. I could feel the sweat inching down my forehead. The pains in my stomach were getting stronger even though I tried to ignore them. I'd excused myself twice already. I can't keep doing this.

"I'm sorry, Mrs. Feinman. I am just not feeling well … will you excuse me again? I'm so sorry."

"Don't worry, dear, go ahead." Sara Feinman looked at me with sympathetic eyes.

I doubled over in pain as I made a mad dash to the bathroom. All I could think was how embarrassing this was—all of it. I held on to the bathroom stall door and made my way to the sink. My reflection in the mirror alarmed me—my face was pale and sweaty. I pressed a wet paper towel tight to my forehead and, after a few moments, wiped my face and tucked my damp, stringy hair behind my ears. I was determined to finish this application today; I wasn't leaving, no matter how I felt. I needed the help or I would be evicted. When I got back to the room, Mrs. Feinman was sitting as I'd left her, patiently waiting for me, looking through some papers on the table.

Mrs. Feinman was the wife of my children's doctor. She was also the mother of a high school classmate named Judi. Judi had been a cheerleader, one of the popular girls. We would talk occasionally during school, but once school was out, we lived in different worlds. Judi would "summer" in Europe while I worked at Walter's, the local hot dog stand.

Mrs. Feinman was the town's welfare housing coordinator. And now she was helping me apply for government assistance. (I wondered, did she think of me as her daughter's old friend or one of her beleaguered welfare cases?) I was desperate. I needed help to pay for an apartment that I had lied my way into while staring at Mr. Martin with a straight face.

Mr. Martin was a landlord who owned several apartment buildings in town. He had a bad reputation; the mere mention of his name triggered horror stories from previous tenants—of evictions for no good reason, of plumbing leaks or appliances that never got fixed, of Mr. Martin keeping money that should have been returned. For a long time, he had a superintendent handling his rentals whose name was Shirley. She was fat and sloppy, made worse by baggy clothes and hair that looked like tangled string. She always looked like she just tumbled out of bed. Everyone knew Shirley was taking money under the table. She would lure desperate apartment seekers into her web of deceit by telling them she could find them an apartment for less money. All they had to do was slip her some cash and they would get the perfect apartment at a "discount." She rarely found them a better apartment, but always managed to take their money. She left a trail of angry renters, and they all had Shirley stories. Her misdeeds earned her the kind of nickname one associates with mobsters, like Tony the Rat or Sammy the Nose. She became Shirley the Sleaze. One of her victims was my good friend Mary.

No one could understand why it took Mr. Martin so long to figure out what Shirley the Sleaze was up to, but when he did he fired her and took over the renting office. I didn't like Mr. Martin. No one liked him.

The first day I met him, I was sitting in his office filling out the rental agreement for one of his apartments. His office was in the basement of his building, a dusty room with old, worn-out furniture. He sat in a large brown leather chair that was scratched and torn. Two of me could fit in that chair.

Mr. Martin was a huge man with a red bulbous nose, mud-brown eyes and a protruding stomach. He spoke with a loud deep voice. He liked to show off his success by wearing a lot of gold rings on his fingers, including one very distinctive one with a big red stone in it. I tried to focus on what he was saying but he had a distracting habit: he would twist his rings and pull them to the ends of his fingers as if he was going to take them off. Then, just before they slipped off he'd push them back onto his fingers.

I sat across from him in a gray metal chair, trying not to seem too anxious. I was desperate to get this apart-ment. My two young children and I were living in my mother's studio apartment. Although I was grateful to not be homeless, it would be impossible to stay there much longer. There was no room to eat or to sleep, no room for the kids to play, and we were all driving each other crazy. Mr. Martin looked up from my application. "So, you have two children."

"Yes. I do. But they're really great kids, and very well behaved."

It was a well-known fact that if you had children or dogs, you were a marked renter. The silence in the room made me uncomfortable, as Mr. Martin seemed to investigate every detail on my application. I watched him nervously twist his rings, especially the one with the red stone. I have to get this apartment, I thought. This would mean a new beginning for me and the kids.

He looked up at me. "You can't afford this apartment. I'll need to see some more income before I rent this to you."

"Well, I'm getting child support." I blurted out.

Mr. Martin put the application down on his desk and paused a minute. He looked at me and said, "OK. Then I need a letter showing how much you're getting and if it's enough you can have the apartment."

"Oh, that's all you need," I said, feigning confidence. "I can have it for you tomorrow."

Child support. What a joke. As if I was getting child support. My ex had decided the way to get me back was to starve me back, so he paid me nothing. I decided I would rather starve than go back to him.

The next day, Mr. Martin had the letter and I had the keys. I had written the letter carefully to make sure it showed there was enough money to get the apartment. Then I forged my soon-to-be-ex husband's signature. I thought about what I had done, but only for a moment. "If someone is starving, is it wrong to steal bread?" I told myself: NO.

I remember the day I made up my mind to leave my husband. I'd walked into our bank to withdraw some money. I noticed a strange look appear on the teller's face when she saw me, and as I approached the window, she walked away. I stood there and waited, wondering what was going on. When she returned, she asked, "Can you please speak to my supervisor?"

"Why? I just have to cash a check." She said nothing more, just stared. "Besides, I'm in a hurry," I said. "I have to pick up my children and I'm late." Just then the supervisor came over to me.

"Will you come into my office, please?"

"What's going on here?" I asked, annoyed.

"I'm sorry, but we can't cash this check—"

"That's ridiculous," I said, cutting her off. "I'm sure it's fine."

"And we can't let you leave the bank."

"What do you mean I can't leave the bank? I just came in to cash a check!" Now I was beside myself. "You can't keep me here! I have children to pick up."

I could see the other customers staring at me and then looking away. It made me feel like a criminal. Now rather embarrassed, I thought, Damn, maybe I should have gone into his office.

"You can't leave, because someone—" Here he looked at me in an accusatory way. "—has been doing something illegal with your bank accounts." He pushed some papers in front of my face.

"This is a mistake. These are not my accounts. They're my husband's business accounts. I don't know anything about his business." All I could think of now was, I had to get out of the bank.

"I'm leaving," I said, and walked out of the bank, ran to my car and sped away. My hands were shaking; I kept looking in the rear-view mirror waiting for a police car to pull me over. No one followed me.

When I got home from the bank, I started to pack. This was not going to be like all those other times. This time was different—no more threats. I was leaving him. Being married to him, having to "escape" from the bank, has made me feel like Bonnie Parker, without the excitement of Clyde or the benefit of the money. Even if I had to scrub floors to make ends meet, I'd gladly do that rather than stay with him. And I wasn't going to fall for any of his suicide threats anymore either.

The first time I threatened to leave him, he called me and said, "I'm driving to the bridge, and I'm going to jump." I was scared. Would he really do it? We talked for a long time, and then he came home. I was sure I had done the right thing by staying on the phone and talking him out of suicide.

The second time he was going to kill himself he didn't say how but assured me he was going to do it. He never did. When I left him after the bank incident I was prepared for his next suicide threat. When that day came, he called and said in his most desperate voice, "I have my head in the oven and I'm turning on the gas."

I said, "Go right ahead and do it." I hung up the phone. I was never called to identify the body, so I figured he never did turn the gas on. In fact, he was alive and well.

It was December when I finally moved into the new apartment. I hated to admit it, but Mr. Martin was right, I couldn't afford it. I referred to this time as "The Winter of My Divorce." A few years earlier I had bought three identical navy-blue pea jackets for the kids and me. I didn't know it at the time, but this was the year that I would hand down the jackets. Mine went to my son, and his went to his sister. It was a little big on her, but it kept her warm. I never had a coat that winter. I layered on sweaters to keep warm. As the sweaters became useless against the cold damp New York winter, I would tell myself: It's December already, winter is almost over. If I were ever going to give divorce advice I would say never leave in the winter. I had lost my home, my car was repossessed, and the kids hated me. I consoled myself by thinking up witty sayings, as Oscar Wilde would do:

"One should always divorce in the summer; it's much more pleasant."

"Always consider any loss as just a temporary loss of conveniences."

Now, Mrs. Feinman was my only hope of keeping this apartment. Again, I took my seat across from her. "I am really sorry. I think I feel better now." She smiled at me and went right back to where she was before I made my mad exit. What I didn't know was that when I was running to the bathroom every few minutes, sick as a dog, she was working diligently on my application. "I think we're going to be OK," she said with a wink. When I heard her say "we're" as if she were part of my mess, I thought: Maybe it will be OK. I'm really glad winter is almost over.

THE STEAK & BREW

IT WASN'T THAT long ago that the quiet, elegant French restaurant, with white tablecloths and a single rose on each table, closed its doors after almost twenty years in business. That was all it took for the Steak & Brew to come to our town. The Steak & Brew was a New York City chain restaurant. Steaks and lobster tails, Beer and Birch Beer, that's all they served. The older townspeople didn't like it one bit. To them, the restaurant transformed our village from a sleepy suburb, where people raised their children, joined the country club and led a quiet life, into a fast-paced decadent Pottersville." Even though New York City was only a twenty-five-minute train ride from our town, it was a world away in character. This is why they renamed it the "New York City Invasion."

For me, it was an opportunity to get a job that allowed me to work at night so I could still be with my children during the day. Finding a babysitter was never a problem; there was always a teenage girl eager to make some extra money, especially if they could occasionally bring their boyfriends up. That was the year I was a waitress at the Steak & Brew.

The smell of stale beer and booze covering the dark shiny wood surface of the bar swirled up my nose as I sat alone at the bar and sipped my coke. It was the end of the night, and everyone was cleaning up; the busboys were clearing off the last dirty tables. I watched Sal hunched behind the bar washing glasses and putting them away. Sal had white hair, a slight bend in his back, short legs and a long torso. He had been bartending for a very long time. He had a nice smile, but he could easily be very disagreeable. He would yell at the waitresses if they didn't give him a drink order "just so." We called him Old Sal, but never to his face. He ran his bar with precision; he knew how to make every drink, and he did it with incredible speed.

My feet were burning and sore; my white sneakers lay on the floor under the bar stool where I had kicked them off. I squeezed my toes together to ease the soreness. I was thinking I'd had a good night. My tables were full most of the night, except for a brief time when Ned made the hostess fill all of his tables first. He made sure everyone knew he was "Head Waiter" and that his tables had to be kept filled.

Ned was half Japanese and half Irish. His eyes were blue, but he had a sallow complexion and thick straight dark hair. He was short and well built. He was almost always in a bad mood, especially when his tables weren't full. Ned wasn't really a waiter; he was an actor, and that's all he wanted to do. He hated and resented having to wait tables for a living. Ned had been in several movies and plays, and made sure we all knew that. Any conversation with him somehow ended up with him talking about his movie roles, even if his part was so small, you could watch the movie several times and never notice him. Talking about his acting made him animated and happy but once the conversation changed, he changed. Keeping up his nice act only lasted for a short time before he reverted to his real self—an angry, frustrated man who had to belittle everyone around him. We all knew it was best to stay away from Ned.

I had a table of twelve men that night, the kind that were big tippers. I was glad it was twelve men and not twelve women. If it were twelve women, they would have passed the check around, each chipping in and carefully calculating the tip. Maybe I would get 15 percent if I were lucky. But when it's twelve men they always drink and flirt, and when it's time to pay the check, one man always says, "I've got it this time," and someone else will say, "It's about time." Then laughter will fill the room. I'll say something like "Oh, so you're the lucky one tonight," and give him a big smile. Now that's a table you know is good for a really big tip.

I could feel my pockets full of bills and change, but I wouldn't know exactly how much I made until I went home. There I'd take out the crumpled bills and pour the change out onto a table, carefully iron out the bills with my hand and place them in piles—ones, fives, tens—and begin to count. But I could tell I had a good night.

I was tired and wanted to get home. I was waiting for my friend Pam to finish cleaning up, so we could walk home together. Our town was safe to walk at night, but it was always better not to take any chances. We didn't live very far from the restaurant.

Sal ignored me as I sat at the bar enjoying the quiet time, when I heard the door open. Three men walked in. They looked like cookie cutters of each other, dressed the same in dark tailored suits, and they all wore hats. They walked towards the bar and stopped, then held their heads up high and scanned the room with their eyes as though they were looking for someone. The man in the middle adjusted his hat and touched his tie; the others waited by his side, and then they all walked towards the bar.

I was still looking at them when my purse fell off my shoulder to the floor. My lipstick, tissues, wallet and a tampon went rolling across the carpet, and landed on the floor, arranged as if placed there in an Andy Warhol painting, waiting to be painted with the appropriate color. I jumped off the barstool and knelt down on the floor. When I started to pick up my things, I noticed the man in the middle was now bending down, his knees in front of my face.

He said, "Here. I'll help you." I saw him reach for my lipstick.

I grabbed the tampon. Thank God, he didn't pick that up. "It's OK," I said. "I can get everything else, but thank you."

"It's no problem at all, let me help you." He continued to pick up more items and put them in my purse.

"Thank you, I can be such a klutz sometimes." I scooped up everything else, grabbed my sneakers and picked myself up off the floor. He stood up too and held out his hand to shake mine.

"My name is Rudy. What's yours?"

I threw my purse over my shoulder and put my sneakers in one hand to free the other, and shook his hand. "I'm Andrea. Thank you for helping me." He smiled at me.

Rudy was young, and he had a rugged, handsome look. I noticed the skin on his face was pocked in places. His eyes were small, his lips were full and he had a nice smile. I never liked the look of a man with a soft face. I liked his face. I liked him.

"Did you have a good night tonight, Andrea?"

"Yes, I did. We were very busy."

"Good. We want you girls to make money. We need to keep good waitresses—that's what makes the restaurant a success. All of our people are important. Well, Andrea, I hope to see you again soon."

"Yes, me too."

He walked back to his friends who, I noticed, never took their eyes off him. They watched him in the way you would watch a child you were protecting from harm. They all walked over to the other end of the bar. Rudy took out his pack of cigarettes. I watched him light up and take a deep drag. He seemed more relaxed than the other two men. They sat on each side of him and kept looking back as if someone else might be around. They looked like mobsters straight out of a movie. I wondered if they had guns on them. I was thinking this can't be real.

Old Sal, who had leaned his head over the bar and was watching everything, just looked at me as I sat back down. Sal wiped his hands on a towel and hurried over to the other end of the bar to serve them.

"Gentleman, what would you like to drink?"

I looked down and tried not to stare at them. Rudy never looked at me again. I could tell that they weren't strangers to Old Sal. His hand shook as he placed the cocktail napkins down, and asked them again, "Gentleman, can I get you a drink?" They answered this time, and he quickly began to make their drinks. Rudy whispered something to the man on his left side, who then got up and went into our manager's office.

Our manager's name was Mr. Macmillan. Everyone called him Mac. Mac was a small thin man, around thirty-five, and married with two young children. He always dressed in a suit and tie that hung awkwardly on him, making him look like a little boy wearing his father's clothes. He was dark Irish—blue eyes, milk-white skin and almost black hair. He had an easygoing personality and was kind and generous, so much so that he became more handsome than he really was. He was in love with one of our waitresses, Cindy. We called her "Cindy The Man Eater."

Cindy was a beautiful girl in her late twenties, with long dark hair and green eyes. She had the perfect nose, straight along the bridge, a bit turned up at the end. It was the type of nose that someone would bring a photo of to a plastic surgeon's office and say, "I want this nose." No one knew much about Cindy except that she always had some very handsome man at her side. She lived alone in our town, but hadn't grown up there as so many of us had. She was friendly and well liked. But she was a closed person; you never felt like you really knew her. What we did know was that Cindy was having an affair with Mac but continued to see many other men at the same time.

When Cindy would leave the restaurant with a man, Mac would sulk. He'd sit at the bar with a drink in his hand and sing along to that Frank Sinatra song "One For My Baby" over and over again until someone would have to ask him to change it because it was depressing the customers. He was hopelessly in love with her. Sometimes I'd overhear Sal tell him, "That's enough now. It's late, go home to your wife and family." At those times, I could see the goodness in Sal, and not the hard worn out man behind the bar.

Mac came out of the office with Rudy's left sideman and sat with all of them at the bar. I was getting sleepy sipping my coke and watching the men when Pam poked me on the arm.

"OK, I'm finished, let's get out of here and go home." She noticed I was looking at the men, especially Rudy.

"Stop staring at them!"

"I'm not staring. Was I staring? Do you know them?"

"Don't ask," Pam said, "I'll tell you when we get out of here. Come on let's go."

Just as we were about to leave, the three men and Mac picked up their drinks, left the bar and walked into Mac's office.

I waited until we were outside before saying anything.

"They look like mobsters in an old movie...the hats, did you see the hats? Who are they?"

"I've seen them before. They always come in together, the three of them. The one in the middle is the big shot, I'm sure of it because they all cater to him. Plus, Sal always stops whatever he's doing and runs like a scared rabbit to get them drinks."

"Yeah, I saw that myself. Sal never runs for anyone, and he did look scared," I said.

"You're not going to believe this, but while I was waiting for you I dropped my purse and my things were all over the floor, even my Tampax—so embarrassing. Anyway, when I was picking everything up, the big guy, Rudy, bent down and helped me pick them up and then introduced himself."

"You're kidding me! Rudy? You know his name?" Pam ran her fingers through her hair.

"I'm not kidding, he really did. And he asked me if I had a good night. He was so nice, he even smiled at me."

"Wow! Nice? Andrea, I don't think he's nice. Like I said, I think he's the Big Shot. All I know is that he's very important. I'm not sure why, but I know he is."

"The Big Shot. You're calling him a big shot. You are so funny. I could tell the other two guys were protecting him, they never took their eyes off of him. I swear, they could be the cast in one of those old mobster movies starring Edward G. Robinson as the boss." Still smiling, I turned to Pam. "Do you really think they're mobsters?"

"Yes! I think they're mobsters. They are mobsters. Maybe low-level ones, but they are not nice people.'

"Well, now that I am so tight with Rudy, maybe I'll become his "gangster moll"—isn't that what they call them?

"Very funny," Pam said. "These people are dangerous, stay away from them."

"I'm so wound up… I doubt if I'll get any sleep to-night," I said

"I hope you didn't take one of those little white pills Stella was giving out …"

"No, not tonight. Those things are unbelievable. One

night I took one at the beginning of my shift, and I was up all night cleaning my house."

Stella was the head hostess at the restaurant. She had two or three hostesses working under her whom she treated like they were her children. She taught them how to greet a customer, and how to make sure that everyone was seated and happy with their table. "Girls, you have to pay attention," she'd say. "If you see that someone isn't happy with the table you sat them at, then change it if you can. We don't want to start out serving a meal to an unhappy customer." She protected her girls from Ned when he was yelling at them for not filling his tables first. I saw her go after him once.

She stared straight into Ned's face. " How dare you make one of my girls cry," she yelled. "Leave my girls alone. They have a job to do. It's not all about you, Ned."

Ned got right back into Stella's face. "You know very well I'm supposed to have all my tables filled right away.

"Don't think for a minute that you scare me. If a customer doesn't want to sit at your table for whatever reason, we're not going to seat him there. Period."

"I'm the head waiter, and that's the agreement, I do extra work around here, and that's my payment, so they better fill my tables first."

Stella stepped in closer to Ned. "Maybe if you were a better actor you wouldn't be here."

Ned's face turned red. He looked like her wanted to kill her. But he turned and walked away.

Stella was a beautiful woman in her late forties, with bleached blond hair, always perfectly styled. She wore expensive bright colored suits and scarves and heavy perfume that lingered in the room long after she left. She was outgoing and talked constantly. She had a million stories about her many husbands and boyfriends. When she was younger Stella had been a Rockette at Radio City Music Hall. One of her favorites stories was about how, to get the job, she had to take a test—balancing herself on top of a huge ball and walking around the stage on it. She was a trained dancer and had fabulous legs, which she would happily show off to anyone who wanted to see them. She was always giving us younger girls life lessons in the form of sayings such as, "To be old and wise you first have to be young and stupid."

But Stella was most famous for being a pill pusher. She had a purse full of pills, white ones to help you stay awake, little pink ones to help you sleep. She was a walking pharmacy. She had come from the city to help open up the restaurant. Whenever Stella saw Mac and Cindy together, she'd say, "That man is going to be in a lot of trouble if he doesn't stay away from that girl."

One Saturday night, when the restaurant was packed with customers, and the lobby full of people waiting to be seated, the worst thing to happen to a restaurant happened.

I was busy picking up my drink order when Pam pulled me aside and, in a panic, told me, "People are getting sick! We have an ambulance on its way here."

"Oh no! Are you kidding me? What's making them sick?"

"I'm not sure. The cooks are saying we got a bad batch of steaks. So many people are getting sick, I feel so bad. Are any of your customers sick?"

"No, I don't think so. Maybe they didn't get the bad steaks."

"Or, maybe they're just not sick—yet!"

"This is horrible. What is Mac going to do—close down?"

"I'm not sure. I think he's trying to figure it out. He called the ambulance because one man was really sick."

"Well I'm not serving any more food to my customers. One of them is a pregnant woman. Good thing they haven't ordered yet."

The ambulance pulled in front of the restaurant, sirens blaring. Several EMTs got out and pushed through the crowd in the lobby to get to the sick customer. By this time, several others were sick. The customers waiting in the lobby began to leave. Stella was no longer the beautiful hostess, but now a triage nurse helping people and clearing out the lobby for the emergency team to treat the sick. The restaurant began to look more like a hospital ward. People were in a panic, scared and worried. All of the staff were helping customers who felt sick and trying to calm everyone else.

Mac announced that the restaurant was closed and asked anyone who had not been served to leave; most of them had already done that. And he said anyone who felt sick should go to the lobby to be seen by the doctors.

It was a long night, but every sick customer was taken care of. The cooks had been right, it was a batch of bad steaks. After that night, the restaurant never fully recovered. There were lots of empty tables for months. In time customers began to come back, but it was never the same as before that night.

After the night of sickness, the staff became closer to each other. It was as though we had all been through a tragic loss. We started to go out after work to party together. We hit all the local bars, and stayed until they closed the doors and kicked us out. One night I got so drunk that I was dancing on top of a bar with one of the cooks. Stella came along and brought all of her pills. Mac and Cindy almost always showed up just a little late. Even Ned would make an appearance once in a while. It was a fun time.

Rudy and his buddies started coming to the restaurant more often to check up on the food orders. Mac was being watched more closely. He felt responsible for what had happened. Nothing was going well for Mac. His wife was suspicious he was cheating, and Cindy was using him to borrow money and then meeting men in the restaurant right in front of him. Whenever she did that, we knew he would spend that night sulking at the bar with the Frank Sinatra song playing. She bounced his emotions around like a pinball, and he let her do it.

One night before I left Mac asked me to get some linens out of the supply room. I opened the door and started to walk in when I was startled by Cindy running out of the room. Her hair hit the side of my face as she rushed by me. "Oh! Cindy, I didn't know you were in here."

Cindy said, "Yes. Sorry, I was just leaving."

As soon as I walked into the room, I saw Rudy standing there. I'd never seen Rudy anywhere other than at the bar or in Mac's office. What were they doing together?

Rudy spoke as if nothing was unusual. "Andrea, how are you?"

"I'm fine, Rudy—I just have to get some linens for Mac."

"Let me help you." Rudy began taking the linens off the shelf and handing them to me. As I left the room, I saw his two buddies waiting for him, leaning against the heavy, metal back door.

I went into Mac's office to give him the linens. Mac was sitting behind his desk, his head down and his hands covering his face.

"Mac, are you all right?"

"Sure, I'm fine. Thanks for getting the linens. I just couldn't go in there myself. Did you see them?"

"Yes…" I hesitated, and then blurted it out. "Cindy was leaving, and Rudy was just standing there. Mac, everyone who cares about you tells you to stay away from her, but you just don't listen."

"Good night, Andrea. I'll see you tomorrow."

"Good night Mac."

Moments after I got home, Pam called. "Do you know what just happened?"

"No," I said, "What happened?"

"After you left Mac and Rudy had a fight. Mac accused Rudy of messing around with Cindy. Then Rudy told Mac to stay out of it, and Mac punched Rudy."

"Oh no—I was afraid he might do something. He was a mess when I left him."

"In a split-second Rudy's men were all over Mac. They punched him in the eye and then started kicking him on the floor until Rudy stopped them. The cooks were standing by with knives in their hands. I thought someone was going to get killed. It was very scary."

"Is Mac OK? Did he go to the hospital?"

"No, he's OK. The cooks put a steak on his eye. Everyone is so worried about him. Stella was very upset and kept saying, 'I warned him to stay away from that girl.'"

Much later that night, the night of the fight, screaming fire truck sirens woke me up. The air was thick with the smell of smoke. I looked out my window, and saw flames coming from the direction of the restaurant. The Steak & Brew was on fire. Our town had a volunteer fire department of devoted firemen, but they just weren't up to the task of containing a huge fire; the building would always just burn to the ground. That's what happened that night. The Steak & Brew was gone, just a flattened pile of blackness in its place. The firemen did manage to save the buildings around the restaurant, but the restaurant itself was a smoldering ash heap.

The next day Pam and I watched them pull down the charred "Steak & Brew" sign and lay it on the burnt out remains.

After the fire, we heard rumors that Rudy and his men had torched the restaurant. The Steak & Brew was losing money, and they were not about to lose any more money. Years later I saw a headline about a murder. The very same Cindy and Rudy had been involved with a man who had been murdered in their apartment. They were questioned and released. We were sure that either Cindy or Rudy had killed the man. Long before this, we'd heard that Mac went back to his wife and children.

After several months of investigation, the authorities determined the restaurant fire was arson. No one had been charged and the burned-out site of the Steak & Brew had been cleared. Now, men were busy hammering; a new building was going up. Pam and I stood at the site of the new construction. We noticed a sign that read "Soon to open *San Souci* Fine French Dining." We just looked at each other.

I said, "You know, I kind of liked the 'invasion,' even though it didn't last long. I miss everyone. We had some really crazy times, didn't we?"

"Yes, we did." She must have noticed the tear running down my face. She reached into her pocket and pulled out a crumpled white tissue and unfolded it. Inside were a white pill and a little pink one.

She put her arm around me and said, "Andrea, look, Stella's pills."

I took the pills, held them in my hand and carefully tucked them away in my pocket.

MR. ANDERSON

STANDING NEXT TO me at the Macy's jewelry counter was a young woman, with long dark hair that shined as though she had just come from the hairdresser. She had a pretty nose and pale skin, and she was with a much older man. Her companion was tall with wavy hair, dressed in a dark suit; he wore it well. They were looking at some bracelets when I heard him tell her to get whatever she wanted.

At first, their conversation annoyed me. I was there to shop, not to listen to them, so I moved away slightly. But then I heard the man say it again, "Get whatever you want." If any man said that to me twice, I'd be looking at a bracelet with large diamonds. Suddenly I found myself at Macy's for the sole purpose of eavesdropping. I moved closer.

"Sweetie," he said, "that one would look great on you." She was thinking about it, I could tell. She cradled the bracelet in her hand examining the diamonds and the intricate details of the design. She turned the bracelet, so it refracted the light; sparkling colors bounced off the stones. Satisfied, she put it against her wrist.

"It's so beautiful," she said. " Oh, I just love it."

"Then you should get it," the man said as he looked lovingly at her. I was standing close enough to recognize the quality and beauty of the bracelet. It was solid gold, with an Art Deco design that complemented the diamonds adorning the top.

Irritated by the girl's hesitation and the "Sweetie-get-whatever-you-want" talk, I looked away. I was startled when the saleslady approached and asked if I needed help. "No, I'm just looking." I waved her off and moved slightly down the counter. I couldn't stop thinking about the episode. What was that young woman doing with an older man? My daughter was a teenager at the time, so the more I thought about their age difference, the angrier I became, I wanted to tell him off. He was probably married, and she didn't know it. Or maybe they worked together, and he was trying to have an affair with her and thought this bracelet would clinch the deal.

"Well, it's obvious why she's with him," I muttered under my breath. "He clearly has a lot of money, and what girl doesn't want expensive jewelry?" I was about to leave the store and get on with my day, when I heard the man say to the saleslady, "We'll take this one." The young woman turned towards him with a big smile on her face and said, "Oh, Dad, thank you so much!"

She gave him a big hug and a kiss. His eyes closed as he returned her embrace and his face took on a warm expression as he bent down to kiss her cheek. The saleslady behind the counter watched with a big smile on her face.

This can't be real. I'm not standing here, I assured myself. I'm home watching an episode of the old television show "Father Knows Best." Mr. Anderson, the Father, had two daughters; his oldest daughter, Betty, whom he called "Princess," and Kathy, whose nickname was "Kitten." There was nothing Mr. Anderson wouldn't do for his daughters. Yes, this must be the scene from the episode where Mr. Anderson buys "Princess" a beautiful bracelet.

Suddenly I felt sick. My head was pounding, and sharp pains pierced my stomach. I had to look away from them. I had to get out of this store. As I walked towards the doors the pains in my stomach became worse; I felt so nauseated I could hardly stand up straight. I pushed past shoppers and rushed to my car.

I had so much to do today I couldn't afford to be sick. What had brought on this pain and nausea so suddenly? I racked my brain for what I had eaten for lunch. No, that couldn't be it; I only had a bagel.

As I doubled over in the car, hoping to feel better, I began to cry. Tears streamed down my face with no explanation. After a while, the pains in my stomach subsided and were replaced with a sense of sadness. "Why am I crying?" I snorted through my sobs. "This is just crazy." But I knew the answer too well. I kept thinking about Mr. Anderson and Betty—that's what I called them now. He was her father, but that relationship had never occurred to me while I was watching them. Why hadn't I thought of that?

Recollections of my own father pushed my thoughts back in time, and the answer slowly came into focus.

My boyfriend was home from college for the weekend, and we were having a fun day talking, laughing and walking around town. I had just turned sixteen, and the memories of the party he had thrown for me were still fresh in my mind. I hadn't taken off the gold heart necklace with a real cultured pearl in the center he had given me that night. The taste of Sal's Pizza still lingered in my mouth as we approached the door to my house; I was still getting used to calling it "home."

We had just moved into a new rental. My parents always rented, they never owned. For as long as I could remember, we lived in Louisa Gardens, Apt 2B. It was a one-bedroom apartment, much too small for five people. I called the bedroom, where all three of us kids slept, "The Hospital Ward." The bedroom was crammed with one double bed and two single beds pushed so close together that they resembled a one large mattress. To reach either side of the room, you had to shuffle along sideways. I can still picture the row of knife slits in the wooden closet doors where my brother released his anger with the precision of a professional carnival act. My parents slept in the living room on a fold-out sofa bed.

That year they had decided to move out of Louisa Gardens and relocate one town over into a rental home— well, it was really only part of the home. I still recall the day my mother took me with her to pay the first month's rent and deposit. We walked into a dark and shabby place on top of a VFW hall. The family that owned our future home also maintained the venue and they lived there rent-free. Apparently, they chose to break up their beautiful old home into rental properties rather than live in it themselves.

Our rental was on the first floor; it had a wrap-around porch with large low windows that looked into the living room. It was still too small for the five of us to live comfortably, so my parents continued to sleep in the living room on a fold-out sofa. My father was far too cheap to buy a home or even rent one that was large enough for his family. He was just waiting for us to grow up and leave.

After living in a second-floor apartment all my life, sleeping in a home with large windows and a wrap-around porch that let in every inch of the pitch-black night scared me senseless. I was sure that those windows were just an invitation for a maniac to break in and kill us all. When I wasn't scared of the house, I would try to picture what it must have looked like when it was just a home for one family, before it had been violated and broken up into apartments for the sole purpose of making money.

As we approached the door, I was still laughing at one of my boyfriend's corny jokes. I buried my head in my purse to find my keys when suddenly the door flung open and my father loomed in front of me. I could tell by the look on his face that he was mad.

"Where were you?" he barked. "Why weren't you home?" Before I had a chance to answer him, he pulled me into the living room, shut the door in my boyfriend's face and turned the lock.

My father pushed me across the room. I almost fell but managed to brace myself on the easy chair; I knew what was coming. Before I could react, my father had grabbed my arm, yanked me close to him, and slapped me across the face, hard. I drew my hands up to my face to protect myself, but the force of his blow threw me across the room. I could see my boyfriend at the glass windows paralyzed with horror. I wanted to yell to him, "Break the window and help me!" But before I could utter a word, I felt another blow to my head. I sensed myself falling and then I was on the floor. Blood dripped from my nose. My father stood above me, yelling in his thick Italian accent, the same accent that sent me running anytime I heard it. If I met a boy who spoke with an Italian accent, even if I suspected he was a sweet boy, I wouldn't wait to find out. No, if a boy with an accent asked me out, I would just say "no" and that was that.

I picked myself off the floor to try and get away, but my father wasn't finished. He hit me again and once more I was thrown to the other side of the living room. I could still see my boyfriend, and I struggled to keep him in my line of vision. I desperately wanted to know he was still there. In an attempt to defend myself from my father's blows I darted from one side of the room to the other like a prizefighter who was losing the match. As I moved, my boyfriend followed me from window to window, like a boxing trainer bobbing his head from side to side each time his fighter took a hit. He punched the window, rattling the glass with his fury each time my father hit me. The glass separated us, but we were together. I could see the pain in his eyes and the cringed expression on his face. Though he never stopped pounding on the glass and yelling at my father to stop, my tormentor never looked away. He just kept hitting me.

I kept trying to get away from my father and promised myself: When he is finally finished beating me, I am going to run to the police and tell them what he did. I was sure this time I was going to do it. After my father had felt he had battered me sufficiently, he stopped. I looked towards the window. My boyfriend was gone.

For the first time, I thanked those large open windows. Because of those windows, the windows that scare me at night, I now have a witness.

I picked myself up off the floor and went into the bathroom to see what damage he had done this time. My head was pounding, and when I looked at my face, I saw countless cuts and bright red bruises. Tears mixed with the blood running down my face. I wet a washcloth with warm water to gently clean my wounds, and I stuffed toilet paper in my nose to stop the bleeding. I knew from past beatings that I needed to shut up and stay far away from my father, so I curled up on the bed and stayed there.

I never did go to the police.

I was startled by a car horn. When I looked up, I saw that a woman was waiting impatiently for my parking space. I sat up, adjusted my seat, and started the car. I looked at myself in the mirror.

Just for a moment, I was in their world, watching a father and daughter who loved each other. I guess fathers like Mr. Anderson and daughters they call "Princess" really do exist after all.

AN ACCIDENTAL MURDER

MARGIE HAD JUST hung up the phone from what she thought would be a pleasant call to her mother. It didn't go quite as she planned. Her mother told her that her sister Donna had just left her house fighting mad and she was on her way over to give Margie a piece of her mind. Her mother told her to try and be the peacemaker and to remember what Donna had gone through and that she just wasn't right in her mind, ever since those beatings. This was always the excuse her mother made for Donna's bad behavior. Margie told herself, "Who does Donna think she is, always telling me what to do. We're not kids anymore."

Margie heard the car screech to a stop in front of her rental on the first floor of a house she had recently moved into. She lived there with her husband, whom she planned on leaving. Margie opened the door and watched as her sister Donna stormed out of the car in a fury, slamming the door so hard that the papers on the dashboard flew into the air and fell to the floor. Donna rushed towards Margie screaming something about their mother. Margie was so used to her sister's rants that her words rolled off her back. Margie's embarrassment about her sister's behavior began a long time ago; she tried to manage it as best as she could. By now the neighbors on the street were watching the scene with outstretched necks. Mrs. Costa, who owned the house and lived upstairs with Mr. Costa, opened the window and stuck her head out to make sure she didn't miss anything. Margie heard Mr. Costa yell to his wife to get back into the house; the window shut, Mrs. Costa disappeared.

Margie braced herself as Donna waddled up to her. Donna was only five feet tall. All the weight she had gained when she was pregnant had settled in her breast and hips. She wasn't like most women who tried to shed the birth weight; Donna wore it with pride. She wore tight low-cut tops that brazenly exposed her breasts. She was partial to cinch belts that pushed her body fat in all directions, emphasizing the rolls on her hips. She kept the belt so tight that it resembled a rubber band that was about to snap. Her long dark hair fell across half her face; she wore black eyeliner with wings on the end of each eye, looking like an evil Cleopatra.

Margie glared at her sister. "What are you doing? Everyone is watching you—are you crazy?"

"I told you that I wasn't going to do everything for mom anymore," Donna shouted. "I've been with mom all morning taking her food shopping and picking up her medication. What are you doing? Nothing! Well, now it's your turn!"

"Don't tell me what to do. If mom wants my help all she has to do is call me and ask, she knows that."

"You know very well mom always relies on me, not you!"

"Oh really! She relies on you? Hah! Maybe it's the other way around—you rely on her. You take her grocery shopping so she'll pay for your groceries. You're not fooling anyone. And when it gets too much for you, you blame me. Why don't you just mount your broom and leave. You're such a witch."

"You ungrateful bitch," Donna stormed off back to her car and sped away.

Margie turned to the onlookers with their outstretched necks. "The show is over, you can go home now." The people on the street turned and walked away.

Once again, Margie was rattled to the core by her sister. She would tell herself she wasn't going to let Donna upset her anymore, but that never worked. Her hand shook as she filled the teakettle. She needed a hot cup of tea to calm her down. She decided she'd call her mom later and find out what this was really all about.

Margie prepared her tea like she always did, the English way, with two teaspoons of sugar and a little milk. She blew on the hot tea and watched it ripple across the cup. She was sitting quietly on the sofa, sipping her tea, when she heard a loud thump coming from Mrs. Costa's apartment above. It sounded like something large fell to the floor. Alarmed, she looked up at the ceiling and heard Mr. Costa yelling "Dissapita!" in his thick accent, and then she heard the sound of a broken glass or plate. Margie knew that word, "Dissapita." It was a Sicilian dialect word meaning without salt or tasteless. Her father would say it to her mother when he didn't like the food she served, just before he raised his hand to her. Her father was dead now, and Margie was glad of it.

Margie stared up at the ceiling waiting for any other sounds to come from the Costa's apartment; she heard nothing for a moment, and then the sound of heavy footsteps coming down the stairs. She looked out the window and saw Mr. Costa getting into his truck.

Mr. Costa owned a landscaping business. His truck was full of tools and had a bright red sign on the side that read "Antonio Costa 's Landscaping Services." Nino, as everyone called him, was an older man with wrinkled, sun-worn skin. He had a red bulbous nose and curly hair that was a mix of black and gray. His muscular arms looked like they didn't belong on his body, but on a much younger man's.

Margie put her tea down and went into the hallway; she stood for a moment at the foot of the long narrow wooden stairs that led to Mrs. Costa's door. She started up the stairs; they creaked with each step she took. Margie knocked on the door and said, "Mrs. Costa, it's Margie." She heard nothing, so she knocked again. No answer. Margie turned the doorknob; the door opened. She stepped into the room with caution. "Mrs. Costa, are you there?" Still no answer. A wooden kitchen chair was lying on the floor; several broken dishes and glasses lay scattered around it. Pasta covered with red sauce was splattered over the checkered kitchen floor, but no Mrs. Costa. Margie stepped over the mess and continued to walk through the house; she entered the bedroom and found Mrs. Costa lying on the bed, her small frame curled up in a fetal position. When Margie carefully touched her arm, Mrs. Costa turned and looked up at her through her deep-set eyes.

Her housedress was speckled with blood. Margie drew in a deep breath and clenched her hands in anger when she saw blood streaming down the side of Mrs. Costa's face. There were several cuts and, and a large gash on her head, her wavy black hair, usually neatly done, now matted with blood.

"Oh my God, your head! You're bleeding. Let me call a doctor, you may need stitches."

"No no no. I'm OK," Mrs. Costa whispered. "I'll be OK, don't worry."

"No, Mrs. Costa, you're really hurt, the cut is deep." Margie looked at it again and was sure it needed stitches. "Please, let me call a doctor or take you to the emergency room," Margie pleaded.

"Margie, I don't want to go the hospital, I'll be OK, really." She searched Margie's face. "Can you do me one favor and go across the street and get Mrs. Fraioli?"

"Oh, of course. I'll go and get her. I'll be right back." Margie rushed down the stairs and across the street.

Mrs. Fraioli was an old friend of Margie's mother; it was she who had told Margie about Mrs. Costa's rental. Every Sunday like clockwork, Mrs. Costa would come down the stairs, cross the street to Mrs. Fraioli's, and together they would walk up the road to the Catholic Church around the corner.

Margie ran across the street and pounded on Mrs. Fraioli's door until she opened it.

"Mrs. Fraioli, you have to come quickly! It's Mrs. Costa. She's hurt badly, and needs your help. "

Mrs. Fraioli grabbed her keys, locked the door and hurried across the street behind Margie.

"That son of a bitch, he did it again. I swear someone needs to beat him up and knock the crap out of him," Mrs. Fraioli said. "I've told her time and time again to leave that man, but she won't do it. "

"I wanted to call a doctor or take her to the emergency room, but she said no, she didn't want to go," Margie said when they reached the door.

"She won't go. If she did, she would have to tell them who did this to her and she won't do that." She turned to face Margie. "Anyway, what do the police do? Nothing. "

Margie knew it was true: the police would do nothing. She had witnessed it herself after her sister was beaten up by her husband. Margie was just twelve, but the memory of her sister's black and blue eyes and broken body was etched in her mind forever. After each beating Margie and her mother would have to get her sister and take her back home to recover. She would stay with them for a while until she was better. Her husband would cry and swear he would never hit her again, but it was not long before he did. Calling the police did nothing. They would come take a report and advise her to leave him. Once an officer told her mother, "She's married to him, lady, what do you want us to do?"

Donna had been married only a few years before she had her daughter. It was only when her husband threatened her daughter that she finally left him. She had to go to Mexico to get a divorce. Beating your wife was not legal grounds for a divorce in New York. The only grounds for divorce was adultery, and even then, you had to prove it.

Margie was sure the whole world was being ripped apart. She watched the news on television in horror. The police were turning fire hoses on freedom marchers and beating them with clubs just because they wanted to vote or to sit at a lunch counter or anywhere on a bus they wanted. She was unaware there were "Colored" and "White" water fountains until she saw them on TV—the sight disgusted her. Young men, guys her age, were off fighting a war in Vietnam. She'd never heard of Vietnam and had no idea where it was, let alone why we were fighting there. What she did know was that the police were ready to beat innocent people but couldn't do anything to help a woman whose husband was beating her.

Margie rushed up the stairs, Mrs. Fraioli trailing behind her. She stopped midway and leaned on the banister to catch her breath. When they entered the bedroom Mrs. Costa was still curled up on the bed, tears running down her face.

"Anna, dear, it's Maria." Mrs. Fraioli said. "Here, can you sit up … so I can look at this? You know head wounds, they always bleed a lot. Let me clean it up so I can get a better look."

Mrs. Costa, now sobbing, rose up on the bed and grabbed Mrs. Fraioli. They embraced each other and cried together.

Margie felt a bit uncomfortable. "I'll go and clean up the mess in the kitchen," She said. She walked back to the kitchen and began picking up the broken dishes and glass that covered the checkered linoleum floor. She stood the chair back on its legs and placed it at the table. She found a mop and cleaned up the red sauce that made the floor look like a crime scene.

Margie watched as Mrs. Fraioli came out of the bedroom holding Mrs. Costa tight in her arms. "I'm taking Anna to my house so she can rest. I cleaned up the wound, and I don't think she needs stitches. One of those butterfly Band-Aids should hold it together so it can heal."

Mrs. Costa stopped and looked at Margie. "Thank you for your help, God bless you." Margie held back the tears welling up in her eyes.

Margie walked down the steep stairs and went back into her apartment. She watched from her window as Mr. Fraioli opened the door to help Mrs. Costa into the house. She knew that Mrs. Fraioli and especially Mr. Fraioli would take good care of Mrs. Costa.

Mr. Fraioli, or "Joe the Barber," as most people called him, owned the local barbershop. Joe, a tall man with a gentle smile, had a large stomach and thinning hair. He was active in the community. When he was younger, he was a volunteer fireman. He was a member of the town council. He raised money for park improvements; one of the park benches had a shiny plaque engraved, "Donated by Mr. and Mrs. Joseph Fraioli." If Mr. Fraioli knew that one of the neighbors had lost a job or was just falling on hard times, he would give everyone in the family free haircuts. If he thought they would be embarrassed going into his shop, he would bring them into his kitchen and cut their hair right there. He knew all the children in the neighborhood, especially the boys; he had been cutting their hair since they were very young.

If he noticed that one of the boys playing in the street

needed a haircut he would shout out, "Billy, you need a haircut. You're starting to look like a girl. Tell your Mother to bring you into the shop."

Billy would shout back, "OK, Mr. Fraioli, I'll tell her."

Joe was never without his beloved dog Murphy. Murphy was a large dog with rust-colored fur, and patches of white scattered throughout. He had one large white spot on his head and one on his nose. He had beautiful dark ears, which perked up when he was happy. Every morning Mr. Fraoli and Murphy would walk up the hill to open up his shop. Murphy would take his spot on the floor next to Joe's barber chair. All the customers loved Murphy; they would stop to pet him and feed him treats that Joe kept in a jar on the window ledge. When it was time to go home they would walk back together; Joe and Murphy were inseparable.

Margie sat on her sofa, exhausted. Her tea was stone cold. She put the kettle on again; she needed her hot tea now even more than before. Mrs. Costa returned home after a few days.

Margie had plans to pick up her mother and take her to lunch. She wanted to talk about Donna, but she also wanted to tell her what happened to Mrs. Costa.

Margie pulled her car up to her mom's apartment. When she entered the building she saw her mother's neighbor, Mrs. Engel, holding a bag of groceries while struggling with the heavy entrance door. "Hi, Mrs. Engel, let me hold that for you." Margie grabbed the handle and kept the door open for her.

"Thank you, Margie," said a grateful Mrs. Engel. "So, you're visiting your mother today?"

"Yes, I'm taking her to the Mamaroneck Diner for lunch," Margie said as she took the heavy grocery bag from her so they could visit in the hallway.

"You're a good daughter, Margie. All mothers should have a good daughter like you."

"Thank you." Margie smiled. "How are your sons doing? Still in Florida?"

"They're fine. Their practice is going well; their kids… everyone is good. They want Mr. Engel and me to move to Florida, but we're not going. I hate Florida, the bugs, the humidity. No—we're not moving. I'm a New Yorker, and I always will be. I was born here, and I'm going to die here."

"I understand. Well, I hope you have a good day." Margie gave the bag of groceries back to Mrs. Engel and walked to her mother's door.

"Have a nice lunch, and try and get your mother to eat more," Mrs. Engel said. "She eats like a bird—poached eggs, coffee and cigarettes, that's all she has."

"I will. Goodbye, Mrs. Engel."

Margie rang her mother's bell. No answer. She rang a second time, keeping her finger pressed on the bell until she heard her mother say, "Who is it?"

"It's me, Mom, Margie."

"Who is it?"

Margie shouted this time. "Mom! It's Margie, open the door." She could hear the clinking sound of metal as her mother unlocked each one of her many locks, then the slipping open of the chain.

"Why do you have five locks and a chain on this door?"

"You never know these days who's going to break in and steal from you."

"Maybe, if you had something to steal, but you don't."

They were seated at the diner and ready to order lunch. "Mom, what the hell is going on with Donna?" Margie asked. "What made her lose it and come over to yell at me for nothing? It was embarrassing; everyone was watching her."

"I don't know what gets into your sister. I told you she's never been right in her head since that animal beat her up." Margie's mother pushed the menu aside. "I think I'll have a poached egg, what are you having?"

"I'll have a BLT. Are you sure that's all you want?"

"Yes, I'm not that hungry."

Margie told her mother what had happened to Mrs. Costa and how she tried to help her.

"That's horrible, that poor woman. I don't think you should get involved, Margie. You never know what he could do to you."

"Why not get involved?" Margie said. "He shouldn't be allowed to beat his wife and get away with it?"

"Let Mrs. Fraioli handle it. They've been friends for years, she knows what to do."

Margie dropped her mother off and thought about what she said about not getting involved. "No, I can't just do nothing," she told herself. She was determined to help Mrs. Costa in any way she could.

Several months had passed since Margie had run up the stairs to help Mrs. Costa. They had become close; she no longer felt like a renter in her home. Margie felt more like she had a second mother. But in spite of their closeness, Margie felt an uneasiness living there. Anytime she heard a sound she would stop what she was doing and listen carefully, eyes aimed intently at the ceiling. She was so afraid that poor Mrs. Costa would be beaten again. She worried that one day Mr. Costa was going to kill her.

It was a Sunday morning. Margie was sitting in the kitchen reading a book when there was a knock on the door. Mrs. Costa was standing there with a box full of red ripe tomatoes, with a few beautiful green zucchinis mixed in.

"Margie dear, here are some fresh tomatoes and zucchini for you. I just picked them from the garden.

"Oh, thank you! They look delicious. Do you want to come in?"

"No, no, I'm off to mass, I'll see you later."

Margie watched as she crossed the street to meet Mrs. Fraioli. They walked together up the hill.

It was much later that day that Margie heard the sounds of an argument upstairs. Once again, she heard Mr. Costa's voice getting louder and louder. She went into the living room and put her ear to the door. The yelling went on for some time. Margie paced the floor wondering what to do. She thought about going upstairs, and then she remembered her mother telling her not to get involved. She didn't know what to do. She opened the door and looked up the stairs, then shut it again and went back to her apartment. She told herself that maybe it would calm down and Mrs. Costa will be OK. Then she thought, what if he kills her this time and I did nothing to stop it. No, I have to do something. I'll go upstairs and knock on the door, and then he'll know that someone else knows what is going on. Maybe that will stop him.

Margie opened the door once again. She saw Mr. Costa's back. He was standing on the landing, facing Mrs. Costa. Margie saw him swing his arm up to hit her when he lost his footing and was thrown off balance. He tried to brace himself with his left hand, his body now turned toward Margie. She stared up at him, and for the first time she saw terror in his face. It looked as though he was just getting a grip on the banister when Margie saw Mrs. Costa shove him in the back. His head thrust forward as he began tumbling down the flight of stairs. The sound of his heavy boots hitting the wooden steps was loud and fierce. In a moment, he was lying at the bottom of the steps, his head twisted, his eyes open but blank. Mrs. Costa saw Margie at the bottom of the stairs looking up at her. She yelled, "Oh my God, Margie, he fell! Quick—call for help."

Within a short time, the police arrived and called for an ambulance. Mr. Costa was pronounced dead. People gathered in the street to see what happened. Mr. and Mrs. Fraioli ran into the house to comfort Mrs. Costa. When the police questioned her about what had happened, Mrs. Costa said, "It all happened so fast. He was leaving and then he fell down the stairs."

The police officer turned to Margie and said, "Did you see what happened?"

COMEUPPANCE

ANDREA STOOD OUTSIDE across from her apartment building in front of the small shopping center. She was waiting for her mother-in-law and her two small children to pick her up. She was wearing her faded bell-bottom jeans and a white tee shirt with yellow peace signs on the front. She tapped the bottom of her new pack of cigarettes a few times, pulled one out and lit up. She took a long drag, tilted her head up to the sky, and blew out the smoke. Smoking relaxed her. Earlier that morning she took a longer than usual shower, and had taken her time fixing her hair and putting on her makeup. Her mother in law had taken the kids overnight. She was thinking, How nice to have time to myself without the kids bothering me.

Andrea was short and weighed all of one hundred and ten pounds. That's what she weighed before her kids were born, and that's what she weighed right after. She never understood why so many women gained so much weight after having children; she never did. People would always say of her, "She's small, but she plays bigger than she is." She loved her children, made sure they had well-balanced meals and read to them every night. She told herself she was a good mother, but she was impatient and drifted off into thoughts of being alone and having a different life. She often thought about her friends who were off at college and free to go to rock concerts or just hang out. She longed for her freedom.

It wouldn't be long now before they came and picked her up; she'd get into the car and back into her role of young mother.

A police car drove by. Andrea recognized Mike O'Neill sitting on the passenger side. "There goes that asshole," she said aloud. She knew he saw her; she wanted to give him the finger, but she kept herself from doing it. She didn't want to think about him and Kerry or the whole Kerry incident. She took another drag of her cigarette and waited.

She saw the car again; it had circled back and was now stopped right in front of her. What the fuck is he doing now?

Mike rolled down the window and stared at Andrea. She squinted her eyes and gave him a dirty look. The other police officer, the driver, turned his head towards the window and said, "Get in the car. You're under arrest."

Andrea looked straight at Mike. "What! Are you kidding me, Mike? I'm not getting in that car with you."

"You have parking tickets that were not paid," the other officer said. "So, we're arresting you."

"Parking tickets, you're arresting me for parking tickets?" she barked at the officer. "That's just crazy, and I hope you know what's really going on here." She nodded toward Mike. "Mike, your partner, is getting back at me, that's what he's doing."

Mike stayed silent in the car and let the other officer do all the talking.

"I don't know anything about that, what I do know is that you have overdue parking tickets and we're arresting you, so get in the car—now."

"No. I am not getting into that car. I can't leave, my mother-in-law is coming to pick me up any minute now, and if I'm not here, she won't know where I am, and she has my children. So no, I'm not going anywhere with you."

Andrea's voice began to crack as she continued. "I'll tell you what's really going on here, officer. I told Mike's wife that he was a no good cheating husband and so now he's trying to get back at me, and that's what this is about, not parking tickets. He has you doing his dirty work for him."

The other officer turned to Mike and said, "Mike, let's just wait until her children come back."

Mike ran his fingers through his hair, put his police cap on, puffed out his chest, ignored the officer opened the car door and got out. He grabbed Andrea's arm and told her. "Get in the car." Under his breath, she could hear him say, "You bitch."

Andrea pulled away from Mike, a look of disdain on her face. "Get away from me, you big ape."

Just then the other officer got out, pushed Mike out of the way, took hold of Andrea and shoved her into the car.

Andrea pushed back and said in a panic, "No, I can't leave. My children, they won't know where I am."

Before she realized it, she was in the back seat of the police car. She immediately reached for the back-door handles, trying to get out. She didn't know it didn't have handles. (How could she; she had never been arrested before and thrown in the back seat of a police car.) She could feel her blood boil inside her, and she felt trapped like an animal in a cage.

"God damn it! Let me out of here!" She yelled at the top of her lungs. "Mike, you son of a bitch. You are not going to get away with this."

Just as they were pulling out Andrea's mother-in-law pulled up. Andrea saw them and yelled through the window, "They're arresting me, follow us to the police station." She was relieved that they arrived when they did, in spite of the embarrassment she felt. Now at least they would know where she was.

The police car drove off, with Andrea in the back seat looking like an ordinary criminal. She sat there thinking how much she wanted to physically hurt Mike. *If only I were a very large strong man I would beat the living shit out of him.*

"Mike—you're a no good sleazy cheating husband. You got caught. That's why I am being arrested." Andrea screamed, "Why don't you tell your partner the truth, you coward."

Andrea turned to the other officer and said, "He's doing this because I told his wife the truth about him, so he's getting back at me, that's what this is all about."

"Shut up," Mike said, turning his head back towards Andrea. "You better shut the fuck up."

"No, I'm not shutting up, and I'm going to tell everyone all about you. I hope you get fired and look like a fool."

Andrea wished Julie were here. Julie could tell them all about what had happened; she knew.

Andrea remembered the first day she and Julie had met Kerry. It was a fall day, just starting to get cold outside. They had put the heavier coats on the kids to keep them warm that day they met in the park. Every day they could, Julie and Andrea would meet at the local park, just a short walk from their apartments. They brought their children there to play together, just as Julie and Andrea had done as kids. That was the day they met Kerry.

They were sitting on the bench talking when they noticed Kerry clutching her light coat around her to keep warm. She hadn't dressed warmly enough for the changing weather. Kerry was watching her two boys play. After a while, she sat down on the park bench next to Andrea and Julie. They started to talk. She had a soft voice, dark hair, and a slightly crooked nose, but she was attractive in spite of it. She said she had just moved into the apartment around the corner from where they lived.

It wasn't long before Kerry became a new friend. Almost every day they would sit on the same bench and watch as their children played in the sandbox, on the Jungle Gym, or just ran around the park together, laughing and playing.

They would talk about their husbands, jobs, apartments, their children. Kerry told them her husband was a local police officer, that his name was Mike O'Neill. They didn't discuss politics very much, but the Vietnam War was still going on, so they did talk about that and hoped it would end soon. They wore POW bracelets, and everyone knew of someone who had died in the war.

Soon the three of them started going to each other's apartments for the kids' birthday parties, or just to visit. Andrea noticed that whenever she was around Kerry's husband, he would stare at her and make jokes. She tried to be friendly without being too friendly. About a year after they first met, Kerry told them she and Mike had bought a house and were soon moving to the next town. Andrea and Julie were both sad to see Kerry move; they had become close in that year and hoped to stay close.

One day Andrea visited Kerry before the move. They were sitting at the table in the kitchen having coffee, while Kerry showed her photos of their new house.

"Oh, it's just great. The kids are going to love that backyard. Now you don't have to take them to the park anymore." Andrea said, with a touch of sadness.

They heard the key in the door. Mike walked in, kissed Kerry hello and scooped up the boys in his arms and gave them a kiss. He was still in his uniform. He was over six feet tall, with large powerful arms and a thick neck. He took off his cap and ran his fingers through his black hair and said, "What a day."

He walked into the other room, and when he came back, he had changed his clothes. He was still tucking in his shirt when he looked at Andrea and said, "Andrea, did I ever tell you about the guy I was working with that had only one hand?"

"Come on, Mike," Kerry said, " leave Andrea alone, she's not interested in your stupid jokes."

"What are you talking about," Mike said, looking straight at Andrea. "She loves my jokes, don't you, Andrea?"

"Sometimes they're funny, but not always; some of them are just gross."

"See," said Kerry. "She hates them. Boys, I told you to clean that up and put your toys away." Kerry walked out of the kitchen into the living room.

Mike watched Kerry leave the room. Then he leaned one hand on the table in front of Andrea and the other hand on the back of her chair. He bent down close to her face. She could smell his cologne. He said, in a whisper, "You like my jokes, and you like me too, don't you, Andrea?'

"What are you doing, Mike? Like I said, I don't always like them." She pushed him away and stood up.

Andrea yelled to Kerry, "Kerry, I have to go now, I'll call you."

"OK, great, talk to you later," Kerry said from the other room.

Andrea walked out the door, thinking: *What is Mike doing? I'm friends with his wife, and he's coming on to me?* She had to tell Julie what had just happened and see what she said about it. Maybe, Andrea thought, she was making too much of it, and he really was just kidding around. She took out a cigarette, lit it and took a drag, then walked straight to Julie's apartment.

Julie lived on the ground floor; Andrea could see her from the window. She tapped on it and waved to Julie to let her in. Julie opened the door.

"Julie, I have to tell you something. It's Mike—I think he's coming on to me."

"Really, what did he do?" Julie said, a worried look on her face.

"Well, you know how he's always telling those stupid

jokes when I'm around, and he looks at me and moves close to me."

"Yeah. I've seen him do that to you," Julie said.

"Well, he did that again just now." Andrea described what happened when Mike came home.

"…So then he whispered in my ear, 'You like my jokes, and you like me, too, don't you Andrea?'"

"How corny, did he actually say that to you?" Julie said, scrunching up her face.

"I know, he's such a jerk. Maybe that's his pickup line."

"Maybe he was just kidding around. You know how those cops are, they think every woman wants them," Julie said.

"You really think so, hunh?"

"I don't know, maybe."

"Maybe you're right. I hope so because Kerry is such a sweet person. I hope he's not cheating on her; she would be devastated. From now on I'm going to be very careful around him."

"Good idea, just stay away from him. It'll be a lot easier when they move."

Andrea kept thinking about what had happened. She told herself it was innocent. He is just a cop, that's what all cops do; they bluster and have to show how manly they are. Mike came from a long line of cops. His father was a cop, and his grandfather was a cop and almost all his male relatives were either cops or firemen.

Kerry and her family moved into their home in the next town over. Andrea, Julie, and Kerry remained friends and visited each other often. For her housewarming party, Andrea and Julie gave them a really nice gift. They were happy for Kerry and would stop by often just to say hi. Stopping by was the way friends showed they were friends, no need for a phone call. It was a friend's code. The past incident with Mike was buried deep in the back of Andrea's mind; she paid no attention to it.

One day Andrea was shopping close to Kerry's new house. She decided to stop by and say hi. She went to the back door, and she could see breakfast dishes on the table. It was open a crack, so she went in and yelled, "Kerry, it's Andrea, you home?"

She heard Mike's voice coming from the basement, "Hi, we're down here, come on down."

Andrea walked downstairs into the basement. There was a sofa on one wall and a pool table in the middle of the room. There were labeled boxes scattered around the floor and several posters leaning against the wall. She didn't see Kerry, only Mike, holding a hammer in his hand.

"Hi, Mike" Andrea looked around. "Where's Kerry?"

"Oh, she's taking the kids to her mother's house, she'll be back soon. Sit down. I'm just hanging some posters—you like them?"

Andrea walked closer to look at the posters and said, "Really— John Wayne posters. I'm sure Kerry didn't pick these."

"What!" Mike said, grinning. "You don't like my posters? Who doesn't like John Wayne?" Mike dropped his smile and squinted at the posters. "How about coming over here and helping me … I want to make sure it's straight. I may need to change this nail."

Andrea hesitated then said, "Sure, OK," and walked over to stand in front of the poster. There he was, John

Wayne in his cowboy hat, looking fierce, with a white bandana tied around his neck, holding a very large rifle.

"Come over here and hold the corner while I check to see if it's straight."

Mike backed up to look at the poster, then adjusted the nail, and hung up the poster. "Thanks for the help," he said, turning to smile at Andrea. "See how well we work together."

Andrea started to move away from the wall. Mike said, "Wait, wait. I want to talk to you."

Andrea stopped. Mike moved closer to her. He pinned her against the wall, his arms outstretched on both sides of her body, his face right in front of hers. He moved in closer to kiss her. Her voice more breath than sound, she said, "What are you doing? Please stop it."

Andrea could hear her heart beating; she felt the flush of embarrassment and nervousness spread across her face. She had to think quickly. How the hell do I get out of this? She bent her knees and slipped out from under one of his outstretched arms.

She looked back at Mike in disgust. "What are you doing, Mike? Kerry is my friend! I thought we were all friends. I need to go."

Andrea ran up the stairs, out of the house and jumped into her car. She lit a cigarette, took a deep drag and just sat for a moment. In the rearview mirror, she saw Mike come to the door and shut it. He never looked at her. She was mad at herself. Why did I go down there; I know I heard him say, "We're down here," not "I'm down here." Or was I mistaken? Did he just say that to get me to come down there with him alone?

When Andrea got home she called Julie to tell her what had happened.

Julie told Andrea, "Don't ever go there again unless you know that Kerry will be there. You always thought he was coming on to you. Now we know for sure he's just a sleazy cop. He's probably been cheating on Kerry all along."

"You're right, Julie I shouldn't have gone down to the basement. As soon as I saw she wasn't there, I should have left."

"Well, at least nothing really happened, so forget about it," Julie said. Almost to herself, Andrea said, "I got away from him, I slipped under his arm and got away. I was so nervous. I could hear my heart beating."

"Whatever you do, don't tell Kerry what happened," Julie instructed Andrea. "Never tell her."

"No, I won't. What's the point? He's such a jerk. And can you believe he was hanging up a John Wayne poster?!"

"Maybe he thinks he's John Wayne," Julie said.

After the incident, Andrea stayed away from Kerry's house for some time. They kept up their friendship with regular phone calls. No one said anything, but it was clear that the relationship between Kerry and Andrea had changed.

Andrea had just opened the door to her apartment when the phone rang, and it was Kerry. She could hear her voice cracking over the phone, and she was crying.

"What's wrong, Kerry?" Andrea said.

"It's Mike, he's cheating on me, and I caught him." Kerry blurted out in between her cries.

"Oh, no." Andrea said, trying to comfort Kerry." How did you find out?"

"I have been suspicious all along, so I followed him one day, and he went to that woman they call Cleopatra. You know her; she walks around in those long Chinese-looking dresses. I think she's a prostitute. But it's not just her. I found notes in his pockets, and he's not always where he says he is. I just know he's been cheating on me for a while now. I don't know what to do. I think I'm going to divorce him."

"Well, have you told him what you found?" Andrea asked.

"No, not yet. I'm trying to figure out what to say to him. Maybe I should just take the kids and leave. I don't know what to do. Andrea…I know he has always liked you…has he ever done anything like, come on to you?"

Andrea could feel pain in her body when Kerry asked that question. She didn't know what to say, but now she heard Julie's voice telling her never to tell Kerry what Mike had done.

"No, he's never done anything like that with me." Andrea lied.

"Are you sure, because I have to know the truth. I just have to so please, please, I beg you to tell me if he has done anything or said anything to you like that."

Andrea thought, she's my friend; she deserves to know the truth about her husband. But is telling her the right thing to do? Will it hurt her more to know than not to know? Julie's words kept running through her head: "Never tell her, never tell her."

Andrea said, "Well, there was this one time when I came to see you, but you weren't home."

She told Kerry the whole story about the basement.

She softened it a bit and told her he must have been just kidding around.

"I'm glad you told me," Kerry said. "I know what he's like, I'm not stupid. Now I have to decide what to do. I want to thank you for telling me."

After they hung up, Andrea felt she had done the right thing telling Kerry the truth. Andrea called Julie.

"You shouldn't have told her," Julie said, "This is not good, I'm sure this is not good. Why did you tell her?"

"Julie, if you could have heard her. She was begging me to tell her. I think she knew all along he was coming on to me. She's not stupid. She caught him going to see a prostitute and found other women's phone numbers and notes. She said she's leaving him. She even thanked me for telling her."

Julie said, "She may have thanked you, but I still think you shouldn't have told her. Well, let's see what happens. What a mess."

Several hours later there was a knock on Andrea's door. Kerry was standing there with tears in her eyes.

"Kerry, come in. Are you all right?" Andrea asked.

"Not really." Andrea walked in. "I confronted him with everything—including what he did to you. He denied everything, especially the thing with you. I came here to tell you...my family is saying not to leave him, you know, I have the kids and the new house. It's my life. I just can't walk away from my life." Kerry stopped. She looked directly at Andrea. "He told me you lied, that it was you that was coming on to him, not the other way around. I just don't know what to think, Andrea, and that's why I'm here, and I want to know the truth."

"Kerry. I told you the truth. You begged me to, and I did. He tried to come on to me, but as I said, nothing really happened. I left, that's all. I know you know I'm telling you the truth, but you have to do what's best for you."

"Andrea, I can't leave him, I just can't. He's my husband, so I have to believe him, you understand, don't you?"

"I understand what you're saying." Andrea put her arms around Kerry. "But I never lied to you. What I told you was true."

Kerry and Andrea hugged each other and said goodbye.

They never saw each other again after that day. Because Julie defended Andrea and told Kerry she was telling the truth, Kerry never saw Julie again either. It was not going to be the kind of friendship that Andrea's mother would talk to her about. Her mother would always say, "Your friends are very important, so make good friends and keep them close, and they will be your friends forever."

The car pulled into the police station. Mike and the other officer got out. The driver opened the door for Andrea. She could see her mother-in-law and the kids parking right behind them. They took Andrea into the station. She faced a large high desk; the officer behind the desk was looking down at some paperwork. Mike and the other officer approached the desk sergeant. The sergeant told the officers to wait on the side and asked Andrea to come closer. He introduced himself as Desk Sergeant Pena.

"Why don't you tell me what's going on here, Miss?" Sergeant Pena said.

"Oh, I'll tell you what's going on here all right. This arrest isn't about parking tickets, that's for sure. This is about Mike, your officer, arresting me because I told his wife the truth about him…" Desk Sergeant Pena held up his hands, but Andrea kept up her rant. "…which is he's a no-good cheating husband. This—all this is about him getting back at me for telling her. I was a good friend of his wife, and he kept coming on to me, and when I refused him and told his wife, he denied it and now he's decided to get back at me."

Sergeant Pena stopped her. "OK, Miss, calm down a bit. Take a deep breath.

"…So, as I said, to get back at me, he used the excuse of parking tickets and got his partner to go along with it, and they arrested me. Who gets arrested for parking tickets?"

Sergeant Pena looked up from writing, and said, "Is that it?"

Andrea said, "I need a cigarette." She noticed her hand was shaking as she lit up, and went on. "I was standing on the curb waiting for my family to pick me up, and then they came along and forced me into the police car. I've never been in a police car before. When I asked them—no, begged them—to wait, because my children would not know where I was, and would have probably have called the police, they wouldn't even wait for them…." Sergeant Pena was nodding his head as he wrote. "Luckily, and only luckily, they got there before I was taken away like a common criminal. They are outside now; you can see for yourself. Is this what your officers are trained to do? Arrest innocent people and ignore the pleas of a mother waiting for her children?"

Sergeant Pena asked Andrea to move up closer to him. He braced himself with his arms and leaned over the desk, "I'm sorry this happened to you. I will have some words with my officers. You can go into the other room, pay your parking tickets and go home to your family."

"Thank you, Sergeant," Andrea said. She turned to leave and gave Mike another dirty look. Before she reached the door, she turned back and could see the angry look on Sergeant Pena's face as he reprimanded the officers. She felt a sense of gratification. She thought, finally he's getting his comeuppance. She loved that word, comeuppance.

Andrea paid her tickets, and when she reached her mother-in-law and children, she smiled.

"What was that all about? Her mother-in-law asked.

"It was nothing, just about parking tickets." She lit her cigarette, took a long drag, tilted her head up to the sky and blew out the smoke. She said, "It's all fine, we can go now."

BLIND-SIGHTED

MAGGIE WAS LYING on the floor watching a television show when the doorbell rang. She watched her mother open the door, but quickly went back to her show. She looked up again only when she noticed her mother's tone of voice had changed. She knew that tone; it was primal, like a hungry animal had just found a tasty meal. Two nice looking young men were standing in the hallway. One of them was holding the first volume of an encyclopedia. Now what is she up to? Maggie wondered.

"Come in, come in," her mother said. "We can talk more about the books inside." It was more of an insistence than an invitation. The young men cautiously stepped into the apartment carrying a heavy black suitcase. Maggie couldn't imagine why her mother acted as though she was interested in the books these salesmen were selling. There were no books in their house. Her mother knew well enough that if Maggie had to do a school report, and needed an encyclopedia she would walk her up the two flights of stairs to the third floor to old Mrs. Henry's apartment to borrow her encyclopedia.

Mrs. Henry lived in a two-bedroom apartment with her sister. There may have been a Mr. Henry, but Maggie had never met him, and he was never talked about. It always took Mrs. Henry a while to answer the door, sometimes several knocks or bell rings before she finally opened the door. Old Mrs. Henry had a wrinkled face. She was thick in the middle and she always wore a printed dress. Her hair was gray and shiny, worn pulled back into a bun, and she always had a smile on her face. Mrs. Henry would open the door and then switch on the lamp. It was always a little dark in her apartment, but light enough to see the fine wood furniture throughout the room. There was a sofa, with carved wood along the top and the arms, curving down to the foot shaped like an animal's paw. The seat was made of patterned fabric, and looked like it would dare anyone to sit down and disturb it.

What Maggie liked most about visiting Mrs. Henry were all the books, sitting neatly inside her old wooden bookcases. She never minded lending her books out, and she would always smile and say the same thing.

"What kind of book do you need this time, Maggie?"

Sometimes Maggie had to do a report on one of the states, or she needed information on dinosaurs. Whatever it was, Mrs. Henry would think for a minute, go over to one of the bookcases, and run her bent finger along the books until she found the right one. She'd pull it out, brush the dust off, and carefully hand it to Maggie, saying, "I think this should do nicely." Maggie never touched the books on her own; she always waited for Mrs. Henry to choose one and give it to her.

Maggie knew her mother wasn't going to buy the encyclopedias. She had no money for books. When she needed a washing machine, she had to use the lay-away plan. The collection man came to the door each week to pick up the payment until it was paid off. It took forever.

Her mother offered the young men some coffee, but they refused and kept talking about how the books could help her children in school. Her mother listened and asked them questions, not about the books but about themselves.

"What are your names?

"I'm Bruce, and this is James," Bruce said.

"How old are you?"

"James is twenty, and I'm twenty-one. This is our summer job, then back to college."

"Oh, so you're college boys. How nice," her mother said. "Your parents must be very proud of you." They smiled slightly. "I have two children, Maggie over here, we call her Mag. And then I have my older daughter Darlene. She just turned eighteen. Would you like to meet her?" Maggie's older sister was in the bedroom; she was not feeling well, so she was resting. She was five years older than Maggie.

The salesmen just looked at each other and then continued to talk about the encyclopedias. They'd taken out several volumes and opened them to show her mother how beautiful they were. They had a special sales pitch they'd memorized and performed flawlessly. Her mother glanced at the books, with about as much interest as a child given a toy that was way too advanced to understand. The salesmen watched as her mother thumbed through the pages pretending to be interested. They were not fooled.

"Maybe this is a bad time for you.... We can come back some other time," James said. Maggie could see they just wanted to get away from her mother. She had seen this look on other people's faces before.

Her mother said, "Oh, no, I'm not busy at all. I am very interested in your books." She put down the volume she had in her hand. "Do they have any books on monkeys? My friend's husband takes care of monkeys in his home. Can you imagine that? I am so scared of them whenever I go over there. I'm always wondering what they must be thinking—" She stopped herself. "Oh, I almost forgot, I was going to introduce you to Darlene. Come on into the bedroom." They made no move to follow her. "It's OK, come on, don't be shy."

"Mom," Maggie said, "They are selling encyclopedias. They don't want to go meet Darlene."

Maggie's mother turned and gave a piercing stare. "Mag, now don't be rude, I'm sure they want to meet Darlene. They're not much older than she is and they are in college, how wonderful is that?" She looked so pleased with herself.

The young men entered the bedroom slowly and looked around with a disapproving eye. It was a bedroom meant for a couple, but it had three beds and a chair that bowed from the weight of the clothes piled high up on it. Darlene was perched up on her bed reading a teen magazine. She quickly put it down and began to fix herself up. She brushed her hair back with her hand and straightened her sweater. Her mother made the introductions, but then became distracted by a loud noise outside. She and Darlene walked over to the window to see what was going on.

Maggie stood behind the salesmen, leaning against the open door, her back pushed against the doorknob. While her mother and sister had their heads out the window, she heard James whisper to Bruce, "This woman doesn't even know how to spell, why would she need an encyclopedia?"

Bruce gave a barely perceptible laugh, and with a slight smile, leaned over to James. "We have to get out of here. The daughter's cute but she's probably just as stupid as the mother." He was looking at the teen magazine on the bed.

Maggie turned to them, eyes squinting, and said, "Why don't you just leave?"

"Believe me, kid, we are going," Bruce said in a sarcastic tone. Gone was the charming boy that came to the door.

Her mother turned from the window just as they were moving out of the bedroom.

"Where are you going?" she said, "I haven't finished looking at the books."

"We have to be on our way, we have so many other people to see. But here …our cards. If you are interested in the books, please give us a call," Bruce said, in the same charming voice he had when he first came to the door.

They rushed out and down the stairs at a fast pace. Her mother closed the door and turned to Maggie. "Weren't those nice boys? I wish they could've stayed longer. I think they liked Darlene—did you see how they were looking at her? That's the kind of boy I think she should marry."

Maggie said, "Mom, they didn't want to meet Darlene. They were not interested in her, they just wanted to sell you encyclopedias. They were not nice boys."

Why Maggie kept thinking about the day the encyclopedia salesmen came to the door, she didn't know.

It had been such a long time since that day. She had moved out of her mother's house long ago and was living her own life, a life she was now trying to run away from. It seemed like a good idea to get away and visit her mother. She was considering moving back to her hometown for a while.

They had lived in several different apartments in the same town for as long as Maggie could remember. The beauty of the houses, the wealth of the town, and the many beaches and harbors formed its distinct character. Maggie felt attached to her town but also that she never fully belonged, like an outsider looking in.

Now, her mother lived alone in a small studio apartment on the ground floor. She had decided to move out of her one bedroom several years ago. She had kept all her furniture; so now everything was crammed together in one room—bed, sofa, dresser, and all. There was a small kitchenette in the corner of the room that she never used. She always ate at the Gold Lake Deli around the corner.

"Mag, why don't we go to Gold Lake for some breakfast?" her mother said.

"Sure, Mom, we'll go to Gold Lake. Is the food still good?" Maggie asked.

"Well, you know, after Joe committed suicide they never could find as good a short order cook as him."

Maggie remembered Joe as a tall, thin man with pasty white skin. He'd worked at Gold Lake on and off for years. He always wore a white cap and an apron tied in front with grease stains on it. He moved with lightning speed behind the counter, tossing plates of food and speaking in diner lingo, like Adam & Eve on a Raft, or one Burn the British.

"Is Joe the one with the horrible wife and he killed himself because she was never happy with him?" Maggie asked, repeating what her mother had told her.

"Yes, that's Joe." her mother said. "That wife of his, she was never satisfied. She wanted fancy things, and he worked so hard to get them for her. But, she was never going to be satisfied. Some women are like that, you know. I miss Joe."

"Why didn't Joe just divorce her instead of killing himself?" Maggie asked.

"Everyone doesn't get divorced at the drop of a hat, you know, they try and work it out." Maggie knew the remark was more about her mother's dissatisfaction with her, since she would soon be getting her second divorce.

Gold Lake was just around the corner from the apartment building. So close that when you walked outside, you could smell the food cooking from the street. It had long ago been a Jewish deli, with great food and loyal customers. Over the years it had changed owners several times, and the food was not as good as it once had been. Now it was just pretending to be an exceptional deli.

Maggie walked into Gold Lake behind her mother. The smell of bacon filled the air, and smoke swirled around the tin ceiling. Her mother was greeted with smiles and chit-chat from several people sitting at booths. One woman came up to Maggie and said, "Oh, you must be Connie's daughter, the little one ... how are you doing?" Maggie looked at the women with a blank stare. Do I know this person?

Before Maggie could respond, her mother said, "Maggie, you remember Mrs. Jamison... she lived next to us when you were just a baby. The two-family home on Palmer Avenue."

Maggie had no recollection of Mrs. Jamison, but said, "Oh, so nice to see you again, how are you doing?"

Mrs. Jamison said, "I'm fine. A few aches and pains, but I am getting old. I hope you're doing OK since your last divorce." She kept shaking her head back and forth, looking at Maggie as though she had just been in a terrible accident. "And now you're getting another one. Life can be so hard."

"Well, thanks for your concern, but I'm OK," Maggie said as she took a deep breath and felt her stomach ache. She was quickly losing her appetite.

As Maggie slid into the booth, she felt something sharp under her leg. Part of the plastic seat was torn and sticking up like a knife ready to tear into her flesh. "Oh, jeez, this seat is lethal! This place is falling apart!" Maggie said. "It stinks of bacon and it's smoky and dirty and—why do you eat here?" she asked her mother.

"It's fine. Why are you making such a fuss about nothing?" her mother said.

"Nothing! This place is disgusting. I don't know how you can eat here." Maggie said. "And who is that woman and why does she know about my divorce? Not only this divorce, apparently, but all my divorces."

"What are you talking about? We've known Mrs. Jamison for years," her mother said.

Maggie leaned across the table to get some sense of privacy and said, "No, Mom, you've known her for years, not me. Are you telling everyone in town about my divorces? Thanks a lot."

"I'm not doing any such thing. She must have heard about it in town. You are always accusing me of telling people things."

"Yes, I'm accusing you because you did it. You do it all the time. That lady didn't hear about my divorce in town… You told her—that's how she heard about it."

Why did I come here? Maggie thought. What made me decide to visit my mother? She had just needed to get away, and this was the easiest place to go.

Maggie had had difficulty communicating with her mother since she was a kid. It made her frustrated and angry, and often more than a little sick to her stomach. Her mother just didn't get her.

Her mother would say things like, "I can't talk to that girl anymore ever since she went to college. I keep telling her she should quit. It's just too much for her to work and go to college. But she just does not listen to me."

Whenever her mother told her to quit college, Maggie would dismiss her and say, "One hundred and twenty credits, that's what I need to graduate and just leave it at that."

Maggie realized long ago that she was straddling two worlds—the one her mother and sister were living in, where reality was what they decided it was, and the world Maggie was living in, what she saw as the normal world. The time she spent with her family, especially her mother, had become more and more difficult.

"I think if you have a poached egg on an English muffin, you will feel a lot better," her mother said. "You had a long flight, you're tired, all this divorce and stress isn't good for you. It's just like when you were working and going to school—you got so sick. I knew you were doing too much."

"Fine, I'll have the egg. But that's not why I'm upset. I'm upset because I can't go anywhere in this town without everyone knowing everything that goes on in my life because you tell them everything. I just wish you would not do that," Maggie said in an exasperated tone before changing the subject.

"I'm thinking about going into the city tomorrow to surprise Aunt Kay."

"Why do you want to visit her?" her mother said harshly. "She's such a witch of a woman. She made my life miserable when your father was alive."

"I just want to say hello. I mean, she's getting old. I have some good memories of her—not many, maybe, but some—even if you don't. Anyway, I want to see the city again. I miss it."

"Well then, why don't you take your sister with you. I'm sure she wants to go. I'll call her," her mother said.

"Don't bother. She doesn't have to come with me. I can go alone." Maggie said. "Besides, doesn't she have to work tomorrow?"

Her mother's face changed. Her lips were shaking, and she was talking fast, insisting that she had to call Darlene. She said she was sure Darlene would want to go with her and that she should not go without her sister.

Maggie said, "Fine, I'll call her when we get home."

Maggie and Darlene stood on the railroad platform waiting for the early train into Grand Central Station. It was a weekday, so the station was crowded with women and men wearing tailored suits and holding briefcases. Cars pulled up to the station, husbands exited the cars, wives waved goodbye. There were a few people seated with newspapers held close to their faces. A young girl dressed in black leotards was carrying a deep black bag with white handles. Below the handle was a picture of a pink ballet shoe and the word DANCE written above it. She wore sunglasses that looked like they would fall off her face at any moment.

"I think it's going to be a nice day in the city, not too cold and no rain," Maggie said. "You sure I'm not taking you away from your job today? Was it OK for you to take off with no notice?"

"Yes, It's fine, Maggie. I really wanted to go with you today." Darlene said.

Maggie rang the lobby doorbell to have Aunt Kay buzz them in. There was no answer. Maggie said, "I hope she's home, because she doesn't know I'm coming. I wanted it to be a surprise."

Darlene said nothing.

Maggie rang again. This time they heard Aunt Kay's voice. "Who is it?"

"It's Maggie and Darlene, Aunt Kay. Please buzz us in," Maggie said.

"Maggie?" Aunt Kay said, "What are you doing here?"

"I'm in New York for just a short time, and I thought I would come visit you. Can you buzz us in?"

The buzzer rang. Maggie pushed the heavy door open, and they started up the dark narrow staircase. The old New York building made climbing the stairs a dangerous sport. Maggie stopped to catch her breath before they reached the last set of stairs. She could see Aunt Kay leaning over the black metal stair railing watching them. The polite greeting she usually got whenever she visited was gone and in its place was an angry snarl. As they got closer, Aunt Kay pushed her body farther over the railing, and bent her head down. "You can come in, Maggie dear," Aunt Kay said before her tone changed to match her snarl. "But I won't let Darlene in. She is not welcome in this house, she stole from me."

"What! What are you talking about, Aunt Kay? What did she steal from you?"

Maggie and Darlene now stood in front of the apartment. Aunt Kay stood in front of her door, guarding it as though some evil spirit was about to enter.

"Just my diamond ring, that's all," Aunt Kay yelled loudly and didn't stop. "That's what she stole from me." Maggie looked over at Darlene. "She came up here with that no-good boyfriend of hers and left with my diamond ring. It was worth a lot of money, and now she won't give it back."

Maggie grabbed Darlene and pulled her to the far side of the landing and glared at her sister. "Did you take Aunt Kay's ring?"

"No! I didn't take it. She gave it to me." Darlene sounded defensive. She wanted me to have it, you know how much she loves me."

"Right," Maggie said.

"She always loved me more than you!" Darlene snapped.

"Darlene! She is standing here in front of me telling me you and your boyfriend stole her diamond ring. If she gave it to you, why would she be yelling that you stole it?" Maggie asked in an angry, frustrated voice.

"I don't know why she is saying that. She gave me the ring, that's all I know," Darlene said, looking away and crossing her arms.

"Aunt Kay, did you give Darlene the ring?" Maggie asked.

"No! No, I didn't. They took it, and I want it back now," Aunt Kay demanded.

Maggie asked Aunt Kay if she would let them into her apartment; they were still standing in the dark landing. She noticed that a few tenants had opened their doors and were watching them. Others were going in and out of their apartments. She felt like the three of them were becoming a sideshow. Maggie walked into the apartment. Darlene stayed outside.

"Maggie, I want my ring back. That was a special ring to me, and I want it back," Aunt Kay said. "You need to help me get it back. Your mother knows about this too. But she's always hated me." Aunt Kay said. "She's probably happy Darlene took my ring."

"Aunt Kay. Please calm down and tell me what happened," Maggie said.

"Well… about three months ago, Darlene came here with that horrible boyfriend of hers, the one with all that curly hair. I think he's Irish. Anyway, she wanted to borrow some money from me, she said she needed to buy a car."

"Borrow! You know Darlene never borrows money. If you give her money, it's gone," Maggie said.

"Anyway, I felt sorry for her, so I let her have the money. While they were here, my neighbor—you've seen her before, Mrs. Cooper—she rang the doorbell and asked if I would come in and see her new grandbaby. So I left the apartment, just for a short time, I left them alone, and that's when they must have taken it. They were the only ones that could have taken it, I'm sure of it," Aunt Kay said.

"Aunt Kay, are you sure you didn't give Darlene the ring? She told me you gave her the ring. Did you?" Maggie asked.

"Now why would I do that, Maggie?" Aunt Kay asked. "No, I didn't give it to her, she took it."

"OK, I'll try to get it back for you. I don't know if I can, but I'll try." Maggie hugged her. "Aunt Kay, I wanted to see you today and say hi. I'm not staying long on this visit. So, how have you been otherwise?" Maggie asked.

"I'm OK. But this business has got me so upset, I just can't think about anything else." She turned to Maggie. "I hear you're getting another divorce. I thought you had a good one this time."

"Yes, I'm getting another divorce. No, he wasn't a good one," Maggie said.

"Oh well. I guess everyone gets divorced these days. Why do people even get married if they're just going to get a divorce," Aunt Kay said to the air.

Right, Maggie wanted to say to Aunt Kay. Some people just kill themselves—maybe so other people will stop talking about their divorce. They'll just talk about the person's suicide, because suicide is so much more interesting than a divorce.

Maggie left the apartment, pulling Darlene from the hallway like she was a rotten sack of potatoes, and left the building. She walked in front of Darlene rubbing her forehead. Her head was pounding, and the pain was making her feel sick to her stomach.

Darlene said, "How about we grab some lunch and then do a little shopping and enjoy the city before we go home?"

"Are you kidding me? I can't eat anything, I'm sick to my stomach from this," Maggie said. "So—are you going to give Aunt Kay her ring back?"

"Why should I? She gave it to me," Darlene said. "And besides, I can't give it back." Maggie could hardly hear the last part; Darlene's voice was so low.

Maggie approached Darlene's denial as she would if it were her mother—since they were so alike. She spoke carefully with slow clear words. "Darlene. You just heard Aunt Kay say she didn't give you the ring, that you took it. Why would she say that if it wasn't true?"

"I don't know why, and I don't want to talk about it anymore. She gave it to me, and that's that. "Darlene said in her defensive voice.

"You sold it, didn't you?" Maggie said. "You sold it, and that's why you can't give it back. Did your sleazy boyfriend have something to do with this?"

"You're just jealous because Aunt Kay always liked me better than you," Darlene shot back. "And because I have a boyfriend and you can't even keep a husband. What's this one, your third divorce?"

Maggie's headache was getting worse. On the train ride home, they spoke to each other only when necessary. Right now, all Maggie could think about was leaving, and it couldn't be fast enough. The sisters parted at the station, without another word said.

When Maggie got back to the apartment, she noticed that her mother's lips were twitching. This was a nervous tic her mother had for as long as Maggie could remember. Maggie had named it the "rabbit twitch." Her mother always had a purse full of pills she called her "nerve pills." Maggie noticed one bottle was opened on the dresser, and she could tell her mother had taken one or maybe two. Her mother's voice quivered. She asked, "How was your trip?"

Maggie stared at her. "Mom, did you know Darlene took a diamond ring from Aunt Kay? Is that why you wanted her to come with me today? So I would hear her twisted side to the story?"

"Your sister didn't take any diamond ring from that evil old lady. She gave it to Darlene," her mother asserted.

"Aunt Kay didn't give the ring to Darlene," Maggie said. "She took it and most likely sold it. Anyway, even if Aunt Kay gave her the ring—which she didn't—she is asking for it back now. Clearly, she is angry and believes Darlene stole her ring. She's asking for it back. Don't you think she should have it back?"

Her mother said, "No, I don't. Are you calling your sister a thief? Darlene was always there for Aunt Kay. Where were you? You moved away from us. So what if Darlene took the ring or it was given to her—she deserves it. That woman was always rotten to me. "

"Mom—this isn't about Aunt Kay being rotten to you or anyone else. It's about stealing. It's not right," Maggie said with conviction.

It was at that moment Maggie knew that whatever she said was not going to change their way of thinking.

She had spent her whole life trying to get away from that strange twisted life, and now she felt like she was being sucked back into it. For her own sanity, she had to get out of there. So, her head pounding and stomach churning, she called a cab to get to the airport.

Before she left, her mother said, "I'm so happy you came for a visit, Mag. Wasn't it fun to all be together again after so long?"

Maggie just said, "Sure, Mom. Great fun."

The plane ride home seemed longer than usual. The next time she needed to run away from her life, she would find a better place to hide.

THE LITTLE
BLACK BOX

BURT RODRIQUEZ, THE victim slash witness counselor, looked at me with his piercing dark brown eyes and said, "So Maggie what did you first see in this man Joe that attracted you?"

"You know, I'm not really sure," I said. "There was just something about him. Maybe it was because he was willing to help me at a time when I was in so much trouble."

Burt was a stocky man. He had dark skin and a thick crop of straight black hair. His arms were muscular and large. He looked like he could crush you if he squeezed you too tightly. His body and demeanor were imposing, but his voice and manner of speaking were calming and reassuring.

He was brought to Arizona from Mexico when he was a boy. He worked in the fields picking fruit alongside his family. Burt would be considered an American success story, the kind they say has "pulled himself up by his boot-straps." In fact, he had a lot of help along the way. After graduating from college, he became a victim slash witness counselor. He was good at his job; everyone who worked there knew that. After a crime was committed, the victim/

witness team, which he led, was called in to work with the survivors.

When I entered his office, I had to squeeze through the doorway sideways against several metal file cabinets. Inside I saw piles and piles of manila file folders all over the room. There was a stack on his desk, more on the floor and several others on a gray metal chair. Carefully, he picked up the pile on the chair and brushed off the seat with the palm of his hand so I could sit there. I watched as he added them to his already overcrowded desk, thinking, I would be embarrassed to have such a mess in my office. Burt was not embarrassed. He seemed to be proud of his stacks of case files, as though they were prizes for all his accomplishments.

Because we both worked in the same office, I had spoken to him many times. At first, it was just a polite "Hi, how are you doing" kind of conversation. We would see each other at staff meetings, or near the coffee and donuts. But as we got to know each other better, we began to talk about our families and the politics of the office. We would talk about how crazy the place was or about the people who had left because they were so angry at the low pay and the insane and often cruel office gossip.

Sometimes he would tell me about the cases he was working on, the murders, and how he and his team would have to clean up the blood and guts after the crime scene was cleared. How he would take aside the survivor or family member and counsel them about what had just happened. How he would try and help them get through this horrible event. I remember thinking, I could never do that, not the counseling part, but the cleaning up a crime scene part.

My co-workers encouraged me to speak to Burt. They noticed I was seesawing between depression and happiness. Ever since Joe lost his job in Arizona, he had been traveling to New York with the intent of starting a consulting business. I was depressed when he returned home and happy when he left to go back to New York. A clear sign of a broken marriage.

At our first meeting, I began by telling Burt about when I first met Joe. That Joe was my second marriage and that I would refer to him in a joking way as "husband number two." I told Burt that just after I met Joe, my first husband had my car repossessed, leaving me stranded. I told him about how stressed I was, thinking I would lose my job because I couldn't get to work. How my first husband had decided he would "starve" me back to him by not paying me any child support, but this had only left me angrier and determined to get away from him. That at the time I had only a high school education and a low paying job. How I spent that first New York winter in sweaters because I didn't have a coat. How I would cry at night from worry that I might have lost my children because I couldn't support them. I told him about how Joe had come to my rescue. How he loaned me a car to get to work. How I took his help because I had no choice, I had to.

I told Burt that I had decided then that I had to educate myself and get a good job because I never wanted to be like that again. How I had visualized the scene in "Gone With The Wind," when Scarlett picks up the dirt and declares, "As God is my witness, I will never be hungry again." It was as though I was in that dirt field with

Scarlett and I swore, as she did—never again!! I worked hard and finished college, got a good job and married Joe. Things were OK at first, but it wasn't long before I realized how absolutely crazy he was. So, after five years of college and a move to Arizona with this second husband, my life was unraveling once again. I felt like I was in a rerun of a bad movie with no happy ending.

Near the end of our first meeting, I began to tell Burt the story of "The Little Black Box." I had listened very carefully to Joe when he brought up the little black box.

Joe told me, "You shouldn't worry too much about money because I have a little black box."

"A little black box," I said. "What are you talking about?"

"I have a black box full of money," he told me. "It's at my parents' house, but no one knows about it but me. It's a secret from my sisters."

He was the only boy in this Italian family, which I knew translates into you are special, and the girls in the family are second. "That's odd," I said to Joe, "why would your parents keep a box full of money just for you?"

"Well, just in case I need it." He said it in a matter of fact way as though it was normal and why would I even question it.

We had to cut our first meeting off before I could finish the story of the little black box, so Burt set up a second meeting. "I think this went well," he said. "I want to meet again so you can tell me more about this little black box."

So now, here I was back for my second meeting with Burt. As soon as I sat down on the metal chair he had brushed off for me, Burt said, "So, tell me more about the little black box Joe had. You never really finished telling me last time we met. I am very curious about this box full of money."

"Well, the box was always full of money. The amount varied, but it was substantial. When Joe needed money, he would just go to his parents' house and take it out. He would pretend it was a magical box because it was never empty of twenty or fifty dollar bills. Of course, his parents just refilled it when he left.

"Before he met me he was spending summers in the Hamptons. He bought clothes from Barney's department store, and he had several credit cards in his name that he never had to pay."

I felt so comfortable talking to Burt. I thought I could sit and talk to him forever about my soon to be ex-husband number two. The hard cold metal chair I was sitting in now felt like a comfy soft chair big enough to put my feet up on, and instead of case files surrounding me it felt like I was sitting in front of a warm fire.

"So, you didn't see any red flags, did you?" Burt asked as he leaned over to pick up one of his files. He held the file up and said, "There were a lot of red flags in this case, but unfortunately no one saw them. "

"I guess I should have seen the 'red flags,' but I didn't. Joe was a spoiled baby who depended on his parents for much too long." I thought, I think his parents liked it that way because he would always need them. I said, "I didn't like the idea of the black box, so I asked him to stop going there and taking their money. He didn't understand why I would ask him to do that."

"When you asked him to stop, did he?"

"Yes, he did—at least I think so. But I could tell he didn't want to, and he resented me for asking him."

"So, then you wanted him to grow up?" Burt asked.

"Yes, I did. And besides, his parents weren't very accepting of my children and me, so that made it difficult as well." Burt nodded. "When we moved here from New York I thought things would be different because he was away from his father. Who was, in my opinion, the reason he was so crazy."

I told Burt about the visits to his parent's house, how they would dress him up like he was a child. He hated the clothes they bought for him, but he would never say that to them. He would stand there and let his father adjust the pants or shirt on his body. His father would say, "Now, there you go, Joe, you're dressed for success now." They were expensive clothes; he knew all along he would never wear them. Before we would leave, he would thank them, take the clothes, pretend he loved them, and when we got home he would throw them out, brand new clothes.

Burt listened carefully to everything I was telling him. He sat in his chair with his head leaning on his fisted hand; occasionally his hand would open up, and run across his face as though he was checking to see if he was clean-shaven. His eyes were always looking at me, and at times I wondered what he was thinking. He asked me a few questions but mostly he just listened.

For me, the most disturbing act Joe played with his parents was when he would brag about how well he was doing in business. It was all a lie. He would tell them about these business deals that he was going to get into, or a business that he was going to buy. None of it was true. They would believe everything he told them and then praise him. I began to realize over time that he never really had to do anything; he just had to act as though he was and he would get their praise. Joe would walk around their house and talk about the deals he was making and his father would say, "Joe, you have to go international with these deals, go international, that's the way to go, Joe." Somehow, I felt that I was sucked into this deception, that just being there with him made me a liar as well. I hated it.

I told Burt the horse farm story. One time Joe decided that he wanted to own a horse farm; he said he wanted to be a "gentlemen farmer." I was not sure what that meant. What I did know is that he knew nothing about farming or about caring for horses. He would ask me to go with him to upstate New York to look for a horse farm. I knew it was a bit crazy, but I went along anyway. At first, it was kind of fun to take a road trip and look at the acres and acres of lush green farmland, with white fences that seemed never to end. I loved the sight of beautiful horses, and the smell of freshly-mown grass that filled the air. But as time went by, and he began to get real estate people involved with the search, it became uncomfortable for me. The real estate agent he found was Pam; she was well dressed and had sold horse farms there for years. Her office always smelled of cinnamon. She took us out to farms for sale, and Joe was his charming self with her, always complimenting her on her dress or hair. She loved it, ate it up. In time, his stories became more exaggerated and the properties he was now asking to look at became larger and more expensive. Soon he wanted to spend all of our free time looking at properties. I knew it was getting out of control.

Since Joe was such a slob at home and needed a full-time maid to follow him around and pick up after him, I knew that if we ever did have a farm, I would be doing all the work. I could imagine what life would be like with Joe on a horse farm. Joe would be in his silk robe (bought at Barney's by his father), sitting in his easy chair reading the morning newspaper in front of a roaring fire, his pipe smoke filling the air, with the smile of a contented gentlemen farmer. Meanwhile, I would be out in the barn, wearing dirty coveralls, sweat on my face, a pitchfork in hand, covered with hay, itching and scratching and spitting hay out of my mouth, doing all the farm work, and thinking only of throwing the pitchfork at Joe.

With visions of me plunging the pitchfork into him, I told Joe I wanted no part of it anymore. I said I wasn't going to waste Pam's time. It was one thing when we were just looking and having a nice day out of town, but it was something else to be deceptive with Pam or anyone else, that it was her job, and she was trying to make a living. He had no intention of buying a farm; it was all just a game to him, just something to amuse himself at other people's expense. We fought about it until I said if he didn't stop I was going to call everyone up and tell them that it was all a lie. This infuriated him, but he did stop. We continued to get calls and property listings sent to us for months after that.

When things got terrible in our house, and we would argue, I would mock his father by imitating his voice, and say, "I think you should go international. Yes, Go international, Joe!" I became an ugly person around him, and I'm not an ugly person. I didn't want to be the person I became around Joe.

I guess the last straw was when he got a job here in Arizona, in a business owned by a woman. He'd come home and tell me he would own that business very soon. I'd say, "What makes you think you are going to own her business?" He would tell me that she was incompetent and that he was much smarter than she was and he could take the business away from her. He started coming home later and later in the evening. He would say he was working late. This went on for quite a while, until I began to get suspicious that something else was going on. Anyway, I found out he was having an affair with his boss. I confronted him about this, and he said it was all in the plan to get the business and he had to do it for us.

"I think this was, as I said before, the last straw!" I told Burt.

"Have you decided to get a divorce?" Burt asked.

"Yes," I said. "I really can't stay with him anymore. He is really crazy, and he's making me crazy. I told him he needs long-term psychiatric treatment and that his father was a big part of his problems.

"I think I made the decision to leave and get a divorce when I knew that I just wanted to kill him." I leaned closer to Burt and said in a whisper, "I wanted to run him over with my car and then back over him again. I know that sounds like I am crazy, but that's what I was thinking." I took a breath and sat back. "Of course, I would never have done it."

Burt leaned over to the pile of files on his table and took one of them out. " Do you see this file here? This is a homicide case. The husband shot his wife in the head. We had to take the children out of the house and place them. Then we cleaned up the crime scene." Burt just looked at me with a stare and said, "It happens all the time, husbands and wives kill each other." He hesitated a moment.

"I'm glad you have decided to get a divorce." From all that you've told me I think you would be better off without him." Burt looked up and ran his hand across his face. "You know, some people are like an onion, they have layers, and in time you peel off each layer, and when you get to the bottom, sometimes they stink." Burt turned toward me. "Anytime you want to speak to me along the way, feel free to come back and we can talk some more."

"Thank you, Burt," I said, "I would like that. It's so hard to talk to anyone about this mess I'm in… so I want you to know how much I appreciate your helping me."

I never did go back to see Burt, but I always remembered what he told me about peeling back the onion. I got my divorce, stayed in Arizona and found a new life.

One day, about a year after my divorce, I was alone sitting in a restaurant eating lunch when I saw my ex-husband's former boss, whom I had named the "Black Widow." From the first time I met her, I felt a strange cold chill. It was a feeling I don't get very often, but I did then.

The memory of our first meeting came vividly back to me. We were at a park for a company cookout for the new employees. She was there with her husband, and we were meeting the other employees. We walked around introducing ourselves and making small talk. My first impression of her was that she was self-confident—attractive, with long black hair; she was slim and tall and had a pointed nose and dark eyes. Joe introduced her to me, and she was polite; we said a few words to each other before she was on her way to meet other people. After she left us I realized that I felt very, very cold; I can remember rubbing my arms trying to warm up. It was as though she brought the cold with her. I'm not a superstitious person, but there was something about her that was unsettling for me. That day I brushed it off as a chilling wind, but later on, I would know that the cold feeling I had was from her.

Not long after the cookout we were invited to a party at her house. From the outside, it just looked like the typical southwestern home, one level with stucco walls. The sun was shining, and it was bright outside, but when you entered her home everything changed. The house was dark and smelled of incense. Most of the walls were painted black, and one wall had an assortment of black wooden African masks hanging on it. I stopped to look at them; I thought they were frighteningly beautiful.

She was showing other guests around her home, so we just joined in. (For some reason, that's what people did in the Southwest. I always thought it a strange custom, since no one ever did that in New York that I knew.) In the bedroom there were more masks on the wall. There was a large shiny black headboard behind a round bed with a silky red cover on it and on top of the silky cover slept two black cats. I felt it again, the same cold chill I had felt at the cookout. I wanted to get out of there; I felt there was something evil in that house. I didn't know it then—I only found out later—that this was where my ex-husband would spend his late nights with her when her husband was away. After that night at her party, anytime I referred to her she was no longer Susan, but the "Black Widow."

And now there she was, the "Black Widow," sitting with another woman at the booth across from me. They were sitting together on the same side of the table; I don't think she saw me. She had a black portfolio out, and she was talking in a business-like way with the other women. I thought to myself; I'm going to go up to her and say something. The question of what I would say kept going through my mind. I could say, you were such an idiot to get involved with him, he just wanted to take your business away from you, he didn't care about you. (Maybe she knew that, and that's why she still has her business, and he's gone.) Or, I could take the high moral ground and say something like, don't you know that having an affair with a married man is a betrayal to all women. Or, I could just walk out of the restaurant and pretend that I never saw her and go on with my life.

No. I decided I needed to tell her something. I paid my bill and casually approached her table. As I got closer, both women tilted their heads up and looked at me. At first, I noticed that she tried to look down after recognizing me. Because they were seated together, it was easy for me to slide in to the other side of the booth and face them straight on. I leaned my hands on the table and said to her, "Hi, Susan (keeping in mind not to call her the Black Widow to her face), do you remember me?"

She said, a bit startled, "Oh, yes it's Maggie, right? How are you?"

I said, "I'm fine, but I have something to tell you."

She backed up from me a little and looked as though she was bracing herself for a blow. She may have thought I was going to yell at her or embarrass her in front of her business friend.

I said, "I just wanted to thank you for helping me get out of a dreadful marriage."

She looked at me, confused and said, "Oh, well you're welcome."

As I left the table I glanced back; I could see her talking to the other woman. I was sure I was the topic of their conversation.

It was funny because I noticed I no longer felt the cold chill of her presence. I now felt somehow connected to her as a woman talking to another woman, knowing that she understood. We both won. She had kept her business, and I had a new life.

Now I had my very own little black box, where I stuffed all the bad memories of my marriage to Joe. It was locked away, but I would open it occasionally when I needed to remember.

THE HIGH OF DECEPTION

MARIA ADJUSTED THE sunshade on the windshield of her car as all Arizonans do in the blistering hot summer. She had burned the palms of her hands on the hot steering wheel a few too many times before she learned about the sunshade. It was Sunday, and she was looking forward to having a relaxing day. When she walked into the shopping center, she noticed it wasn't very crowded, at least not yet. Maria didn't have anything in particular she wanted to buy. She just wanted to get out of the house for a while and walk in the cool air conditioning. But mostly she needed a distraction—anything to stop thinking about the ugly and upsetting scene at work with Sandy.

She walked through the center looking at the window displays; nothing particularly appealed to her. She preferred small boutiques that sold quality clothing with a unique look. She wore mostly fitted clothes; they looked better on her small frame.

One store after another had displays of cheap-looking tops and dresses pinned on lifeless bodies. If the window mannequins could come to life, they would shout, "Get this junk off of me!" She grimaced. Who buys these clothes?

She walked over to a long display table. A few people were looking at the books and magazines that practically toppled off the table. She had just picked up one of the books and was reading the inside flap when she noticed him.

His head was bald but he was young, too young to be naturally bald. She figured he must have shaved his head. He had a long face, and a scar just above his right eye, but he was quite good looking. Tattoos adorned his muscular arms from his shoulder to his wrist. Maria wasn't like most people her age; tattoos didn't alarm her and she found them fascinating. She loved art, and to her this was just another art form. His sleeveless t-shirt was noticeable underneath the black leather vest. The vest had round metal buttons on each side, under which were small ivory bone decorations in the shape of a skull. Each side of the vest had long leather ties that hung down. In the middle was a silver link chain. His jeans were black. She noticed him in such detail because he was standing so close to her. His closeness made her uncomfortable, so she backed away and moved to the other side of the table. Standing across from him, she could see his face better. She looked straight at him; he looked back at her, with intense blue eyes. His face looked familiar. She looked away and browsed the books a little while longer before moving on to the other stores.

Maria stepped into a clothing store and tried on a few tops. Nothing seemed to fit. As she was leaving the store, she saw him again, the leather-vested guy. There he is again. How strange, she thought, and tried to toss it off with a little shake of her head.

She walked on for quite a while. The mall was noisy now and crowded with shoppers. The smell of a hot salty pretzel overwhelmed her; she had to have one. She was biting into the pretzel when her napkin dropped. "Oh shit!" she said aloud and bent down to pick it up. When she stood up, there he was, right in front of her, staring at her. He scared her. Maria backed away from him, turned around and walked away. She could hear her heart pounding; her hands were shaking. Who the hell is this guy? Could he be following me?

Maria was a New Yorker in heart and mind; she wasn't going to let this guy get the better of her. She had learned to always be on guard for any danger, especially when she left the suburbs and visited New York City. It was the era when "squeegee men" came up to the cars and cleaned the windows, asking for money. This was when women who didn't hide their jewelry were often assaulted and robbed. The police had warned women not to wear jewelry, but if they did, they should turn their rings into the palms of their hands. Maria always said that if anyone tried to harm her, she would fight them off as best as she could, even if she lost.

Maria was determined to find out what was going on. Was he following her or was she just being paranoid? She would keep walking and get as far away from him as she could while keeping a keen eye out for him. Maybe he was following her, but now she felt like she was following him, too. She went into a candy store and looked at the chocolates and sugar cookies on display. She didn't want any sweets but thought she should at least buy something, so she bought a sugar cookie, wrapped it in a napkin and stuffed it in her purse. When she left the store, he was nowhere in sight so she relaxed a bit. And then suddenly, he was beside her. Where had he come from? How had she missed seeing him? What was this cat and mouse game he was playing? He didn't look at her; he just walked past. Now she was sure he was following her. She tried to keep calm, but her body was shaking to her bones, she could hear the pounding of her heart. It was time to plan an escape.

Maria's mind was churning with thoughts of how to get away from him. She felt sure that with a carefully thought out plan she could get away safely. Her plan was to hide in a store close to the exit door, and watch for him. If she saw him, she'd wait until he wasn't looking her way and run to her car as fast as she could. There was a small bookstore, close to the exit. Perfect. Maria walked through the store making sure he wasn't there, and found a small corner nook filled with books. She squeezed into the space and positioned herself so she could see who entered the store and still be hidden. She waited; she was sure he would show up. The time passed slowly; she watched shoppers browse the books and make their purchases. Two young girls were running around the store. One of them, clearly the leader, yanked the other one towards the Disney books, and they opened up the book with a princess on the cover. Maria watched them as they giggled and turned each page, and for a moment she slipped into their carefree fantasy world.

She began to feel silly standing there, pretending to be looking for a book, waiting for this guy in a vest. That face of his, with that scar above his eye—he looked so familiar, but she couldn't place him. "Dammit!" she said to herself in a whisper. "What am I doing hiding in a bookstore? This is just crazy!"

This stalker was robbing her of the quiet, peaceful Sunday she so desperately needed. Instead, she was getting ready to carry out her escape. Back in her head were the thoughts of Sandy, her job, and her decision, which she now thought to be a rash one, to move to Arizona.

For as long as Maria could remember she had always wanted to leave New York. She hated the cold, damp winters and the hot, sweaty summers. She was a head sweater. Her hair was always dripping wet in the summer, making her look like a damp dog. In her mind, any reason to leave New York was a good reason. Of course, she had never lived anywhere else until now. She would tell anyone who would listen, "Just because my grandmother stepped off the boat from Italy in New York doesn't mean I have to live here forever. "

Now she remembered her first day at work. She'd left her closet a mess that morning, her discarded outfits, dresses, skirts and blouses scattered over the floor as she tried them on and took them off one by one. She would clean up the mess later. She decided on a long black skirt, a lightweight jacket and a silk top. She brushed back her long dark hair and clipped it back for a more professional look. It was winter, and there was a desert morning chill in the air, but nothing like the cold, bitter winters in New York.

Maria was hired as a manager to fix the many problems in the misdemeanor department. She had never been a manager before. One idea in particular excited her: the thought of working on the right side of the law, the prosecution, helping to put the bad guys away. Criminal law would be new to her, but her degree and training made her feel confident she could handle any area of law. She'd always done well in interviews, and was usually offered the job or even a better one. This interview went as well as usual; she gave thorough answers to everything they threw at her. She had barely walked into her house and put her purse down before the phone rang and they offered her the job.

Maria pulled down the car mirror to look at herself and brush the crumbs off her mouth. She had grabbed a piece of toast to eat on her way to work because changing all her outfits made her late. As she waited for the elevator, adjusting her skirt and jacket, she noticed two women standing next to her staring at her. She was wiping her mouth, to catch any stray crumbs, when she realized they were staring at her outfit. She gave them a polite smile and looked away. She noticed they were dressed in bright colors—pinks and blues—and their shoes matched the color of the outfit. They wore bangle bracelets of the same color, too. Maria couldn't believe it. Am I back in the 1950s? This was the 1980s—at least in New York. The women continued to stare at her and then look at each other as the elevator moved slowly up to the fifth floor. Now Maria felt annoyed and just wanted to get away from these color matching, bangle bracelet women. They all got off on the fifth floor. Oh God! I hope I don't have to work with these women.

Maria stepped up to the counter with the sliding glass window and introduced herself. The bangle bracelet women walked through the door into the office. Maria waited until a masculine looking woman with short dark hair and bright blue eyes approached her. It was Rickie, from the interview. She was dressed in black slacks and a tee shirt, like she was going to a ballgame. Maria smiled.

"Hi, I'm so happy that finally, a real paralegal will be working here. I've been waiting for a long time for this."

"It's good to see you again," Maria said." I'm looking forward to working here."

Rickie was smart; during the interview, she asked most of the questions, and often nodded in agreement with Maria's answers. Rickie guided Maria through a flurry of paperwork, gave her a badge to wear, and then warned her about the unmanageable, dysfunctional misdemeanor department she was hired to fix. In the interview, Maria gathered that no one seemed to know why the department didn't work; they just knew it didn't and were desperate for someone to mend it.

Rickie walked Maria to her work area and told her a woman named Kathy would be there soon to introduce her to everyone. Kathy was the woman Maria would replace. "Good luck, I'll check in on you in a few days," Rickie said and smiled. "I'm planning on getting you out of this department as fast as I can, so we can work together."

Nausea seized the pit of her stomach when Maria saw her workspace. It wasn't an office like she imagined it would be. An old dirty wooden desk sat lopsided on the floor, with particles of wood peeling off its sides. It was in a dingy, dark hallway with another filthy desk practically on top of it. There was an odor, like the smell of dirty sneakers stuffed under a bed in a teenage boy's room. Everything about this disgusting place made her skeeve. She was already missing her New York office, the beautiful teakwood desk, and large windows with sunlight shining through. The rich insurance company she worked for would never have expected her to work in this filth. She had a secretary, a sweet young girl named Linda, who cried when Maria told her she was leaving. It was clear she wasn't in New York anymore. Or Kansas, for that matter.

Maria heard the click of high heels and the clanging of those damned bangle bracelets. A woman fluttered around laughing and talking to all the other people in the office. It was the pink bangle bracelet lady from the elevator.

The woman approached Maria, "Hi, I'm Kathy, Kathy with a K, not a C. I saw you in the elevator," Kathy with a K said. " You're taking over my job, so I'm going to show you around and train you."

"Hi Kathy, it's nice to meet you, I'm Maria." She couldn't imagine how this flighty woman could possibly train her.

"Yes, I know, they told me all about you. I'll show you around and introduce you to all our baby attorneys."

"Baby attorneys?" Maria said.

"Yes, that's what we call them here. They start out in our misdemeanor department and then eventually move up to the other floors to work on the felony cases. Most of them have just graduated from law school, and it really shows," Kathy said as she picked up a donut and stuffed it into her mouth. Maria noticed that Kathy with a K had a quirky manner of speaking; she didn't say her words, she would sing them. Maria, annoyed by this, had visions of her breaking into a song at any moment.

As they walked together through the department, Kathy smiled and was friendly to everyone in the department. And then she turned to Maria and in a whispered tone told her all the office gossip, personal and professional, leaving no one out. She readily shared who she thought was a "bitch" and who she thought was nice.

"This is Sandy, our newest employee besides you. She's working on background checks, and she's a wiz with this new computer. Maria will be your new manager when I leave," Kathy with a K said with a frown on her face.

"Hi Sandy, it's nice to meet you," Maria said politely.

"Hi," Sandy said as she looked at Maria with suspicious eyes, and kept working.

Sandy was a woman in her mid-thirties with a round face, dark hair and brown eyes. She wore heavy foundation makeup and bright blue eye shadow that sparkled beneath her glasses. She wasn't overweight, but a bit thick in the middle. A framed photo on Sandy's desk showed her with her arms wrapped around her two children, her husband standing tall in his Marine uniform and hat. Kathy told her that Sandy was once in the Navy. Maria would have guessed this anyway. There was just something about Sandy that screamed "military."

It became apparent to Maria that Kathy with a K

would never be able to teach her anything other than office gossip. She knew she would just have to wait for her to leave and learn the job herself. Her assessment of the department was that it was a mess. Attorneys ran around the office looking for forms, complaining about no help and dragging cardboard boxes full of files to court. There were too many cases, not enough attorneys and no organization.

Maria set out to fix the department as best as she could. She began by trying to organize the closet that held all of the office forms. What she found was a dirty, dusty closet that had not been cleaned out for years and forms that were piled in a corner, presumed to be missing. Maria was on the floor of the closet, with a bucket of soapy water cleaning, when Marilyn, a new attorney, burst into the closet in a frenzied state.

"Is there anyone here who can make copies for me?" Marilyn barked at Maria.

"No, I'm sorry you're going to have to make them yourself," Maria said, wiping the sweat from her forehead with the back of her hand.

"You know, I didn't go to law school to make copies, I'm an attorney." Marilyn snapped.

Maria wasn't going to respond to this on her knees. She stood up and stared at Marilyn. "I didn't go to college for five years getting my degree to clean out a hot dirty closet either. If I can clean out this filthy closet so you can have the forms you need, then you can make your own copies."

Marilyn stormed out, talking to herself, "I need to get out of here and work for a private law firm." No one would miss her if she left, Maria thought.

As the time passed, Maria became more comfortable in the job. She was making changes in procedures, but with every change came the grumbling and huddling of resistance. Most of the staff were older women who had been doing things the same way for years. Their leader and designated spokesperson was Gloria, a short woman, fifty-ish with black and gray hair. It was Gloria around whom everyone gathered in the morning, bringing her coffee and donuts. Whenever someone had a problem, she went to Gloria for solutions. She was in charge of keeping track of everyone's birthday, sending cards around to be signed, and collecting money for office parties. When Maria approached Gloria with a procedural change, she decided it was time to speak up for the group.

"I don't like these changes at all," Gloria asserted. "It's not going to work, the old way was better." Maria listened patiently. "Mrs. Miller taught us how to do it, it's the best way, and we've been doing it like this for years."

Maria took a deep breath. "Gloria, who is Mrs. Miller?"

"Mrs. Miller was our manager, we all loved her. She worked out the best way to do everything."

"Oh. I never heard of Mrs. Miller. When did she leave?" Maria asked with some curiosity.

"Well, now, let's see…. Mrs. Miller retired about ten years ago. Soon after that, her husband died, and she moved away."

"Gloria, that was a very long time ago, and the world has changed since then. I'm sorry, but we need to modify the procedures so I would appreciate your help with new ideas." Maria knew that if she could get Gloria on board, everyone else would follow.

"OK, well then we'll just have to do it your way," Gloria said as she rolled her eyes and ran off to huddle with the other workers.

Maria couldn't understand why they couldn't see that she was trying to make their job easier. No matter how Maria tried to involve the staff or enlist their help with changes, they resented it. With every improvement Maria tried to make, fierce resistance followed.

Everyone in the office was excited about Cinco de Mayo. To celebrate, the entire office staff gathered at their favorite Mexican restaurant for lunch. As Maria struggled to find something on the menu she could eat that didn't set her mouth on fire, she overheard several women talking about a person named Wally Olson. They were praising him and everyone seemed to know who he was. They spoke about him in hushed tones, as though he was a god.

Maria asked. "Who is Wally Olson?" Suddenly everyone was staring at Maria with bemused looks on their faces.

"You don't know who Wally Olson is!!" They all burst out into loud laughter.

"No, who is he?" Maria asked, annoyed and embarrassed at the same time.

"He's just the most famous basketball coach there is."

The laughter and the embarrassment of asking that question sunk into Maria like a sword, but that quickly turned into indignation. Who are these people? Who cares about some stupid basketball coach named Wally Olson? Why didn't they know he isn't actually famous?

What Maria did care about was that she couldn't get a decent pizza in this God forsaken desert, or a deli sandwich that didn't taste like cardboard. She wasn't able to talk to anyone about things she felt were interesting. She had decided that this place was dull and boring. Even more important, it was Fashion Dead. Everyone wore outdated clothes and dressed in cowboy hats and boots. They watched parades with no music, while girls in bright-colored, fringed outfits rode horses and threw candy on the streets for children to run and pick up. If Maria had lunch with someone at work they always wanted to go to a Mexican restaurant. She hated Mexican food. She felt sure that she would never understand these people and they would never understand her.

In spite of all this, Maria wanted to succeed in her job. She was hired to manage and fix the problems in the department, and she was determined to get it done. She worked closely with Sandy, to make sure that every person in every case had a criminal history background check. Maria would bounce her ideas about procedural changes off Sandy. She wasn't resistant to change; she was creative and smart and efficient. Maria enjoyed working with her; the dysfunctional department she had inherited began to improve.

At times Maria felt she had a forged a personal bond with Sandy, and then other times she felt completely shut out from her. Sandy's mood could quickly turn from very friendly to cold and distant. She made a habit of always being the first person in the office in the morning. At first Maria thought this was because she was ambitious and hardworking, only to find out later this wasn't the reason at all.

Sandy always wore a long-sleeved shirt, even when it

was scorching hot outside. At times her face foundation was so thick it looked as though you could grab a corner and peel it off in one piece. One day the air conditioning in the office was broken; everyone was sweating and dragging out the old fans to try and stay cool. They considered closing the office early if the A.C. took too long to repair. Maria was worried about her staff and kept watching to make sure everyone was doing OK. She wet a paper towel and put it on her forehead. People fanned their faces, while others stood in front of the fans pulling at their clothes to get the cool air inside. Maria approached Sandy to see how she was doing. She was wiping the sweat from her face. Her foundation began to rub off, revealing black and blue marks under her eyes, on her cheeks, and even her neck. It was then Maria realized that Sandy was concealing her bruises. And those long-sleeved shirts—what could they be hiding?

Maria decided to wait until the next day to talk to Sandy about her bruises. She sat down next to Sandy and quietly asked her about them. Sandy joked and said, "Oh those, I was playing with the kids and fell, that's all." Soon other people in the office started saying they thought Sandy was being abused. Each time Maria passed Sandy's desk she would look at that happy family photo, stare at her husband in his uniform and hat, feeling an intense dislike for him. Was he beating her?

It was a Friday morning, and Maria was exhausted from not sleeping the night before. She was looking forward to an easy day at work. She had just plopped down in her chair when a sweet smell filled her nose. A teenager in the sixties, she knew that smell: it could only be marijuana. She walked around the offices sniffing, trying to find out where it was coming from. When Maria approached Sandy at her desk, she knew she didn't have to look any further; the smell was so much stronger now.

"Sandy, I smell marijuana, and it's strongest when I'm near you. Did you smoke a joint in here?" Maria asked.

"What? No!" Sandy said emphatically. "I never smoke marijuana. Why are you asking me?"

"I'm asking you because this office stinks of marijuana and you're the only other person here, and you reek of it. So, I'm asking you again, did you smoke marijuana in this office?"

"No, I didn't," Sandy said, and angrily turned her head and went back to her work.

"OK, Sandy, I'm telling you right now, just so you understand. This is the County Attorney's office, and we prosecute people for smoking marijuana—it's against the law. You have to stop smoking pot in the office," Maria said. "If you're having problems at home, please tell me. We can get you help."

Sandy stayed quiet and looked up at Maria, "I'm fine. I just need to get back to work."

Maria walked away in disbelief. How could this smart woman do something so stupid? She decided to let it go, and she hoped Sandy got the message. But not long after that first incident it happened again and then again. Maria tried several times to get Sandy to open up about the abuse and the pot smoking, but nothing worked. Sandy was in denial, and nothing could shake her from it.

One morning Mr. Peter W. Cranston, the county attorney, came to speak to Maria. As they walked through the office discussing the changes she had made, Maria could smell the lingering scent of marijuana in the air. That was when she decided she couldn't allow this to continue. She would have to talk to her manager Barbara about Sandy's pot smoking.

Barbara was a tall, thin, pretty blond who was always on a diet. When she sat down her thick legs stuck out from her skirt. They looked strange, as though they belonged to someone else; they didn't appear to fit with the rest of her thin frame. She kept a water bottle with her at all times and a box of raisins on her desk. As she spoke, she would reach into the box, pull out a wad of sticky raisins, pop them one at a time in her mouth and nibble them. She seemed to be always hungry. Barbara would disappear from work for one or two weeks at a time. It was common knowledge that she was, once again, in treatment for her addictions.

"Barbara, I need to do something about Sandy," Maria said. "She's smoking pot in the office. I know it's hard to believe, but she's doing it."

"Oh! Well, what do you want to do? Do you want to fire her?" Barbara said as she stuffed more raisins in her mouth. "If you do fire her, first find out who her connection is, mine just got arrested. Oh! You know I'm only kidding," Barbara said with a coy smile.

Maria just stared at Barbara. She had expected her to be more outraged.

Barbara said, "I know, let's go to lunch, and you can tell me more about what happened. We'll figure out what to do."

Maria sat across from Barbara, watching her sip her Margarita and nibble on chips and salsa, the same way she nibbled on her raisins, waiting for lunch to arrive. Maria began telling Barbara about the many times she had caught Sandy smoking pot and told her to stop, but that it continued. She told her about the suspected abuse and Sandy's denial.

"I just finalized my divorce yesterday," Barbara blurted out. "I'm in a good mood, so lunch is my treat."

"Oh, well thank you. I'm sorry about your divorce," Maria said sympathetically.

"Don't be. It was my fault." Barbara said and took another sip of her Margarita," I'm a sex addict. I cheated on him. I cheated on all my husbands."

Barbara's candid admission made Maria uncomfortable. At the same time, she did admire her for her honesty.

"I think a divorce can be a new beginning," Maria said.

"I guess so. I'm trying to figure it all out with my therapist; we're trying to tap into my inner child. She's sure it's my inner child crying out for affection. I have these dreams of being molested, so we're exploring that as well."

Blah, Blah, Blah, Barbara went on and on. Maria didn't want to hear about Barbara's inner child, her sex addiction, or her dreams of molestation, real or imagined; she wanted to discuss what to do about Sandy.

"So, Barbara, I can't keep letting Sandy smoke pot in the office. I've already warned her, and it's continued. I think she needs to be fired."

"OK, you can do it," Barbara said. "She's still on probation, so all you have to do is tell her, it's that easy.

You don't even have to give her a reason. But, you have to do it quickly because when she comes off of probation, it gets complicated."

"So I can just fire her? Tomorrow's Friday, should I do it tomorrow?" Maria asked, but at the same time wishing that Barbara would do it.

"Sure, tomorrow's good. When you tell Sandy, she has to see Anne, hand in her badge and sign out. You will have to go with her to make sure she actually does it and then leaves the building."

Barbara continued to talk about her addictions through lunch. Maria sat there and smiled a few times while Barbara was talking, but she didn't hear another word she said. All she could think about was how to go about firing Sandy. She felt it was the right thing to do, but now she actually had to do it.

"It's late." Barbara looked at her watch. "We better get back to work."

Maria came into the office the next morning after a sleepless night. She was upset at the thought of having to fire Sandy. She liked her, they worked well together, and she had never fired anyone before. She would wait until the end of the day and use one of the empty attorney's offices so it would be private. Sandy was sitting at her desk when Maria approached her.

"Sandy, could you come into the office with me? I need to speak to you," Maria said.

"Why, what's this about?" Sandy asked.

"I just need to speak to you, in private."

"Why can't you talk to me here, I'm working."

Maria was annoyed and sharpened her tone. "Sandy, I

want you to come into the office now. I need to speak to you."

Sandy threw the papers in her hand on the desk, stood up, and walked defiantly into the office.

They sat across from each other. Maria began, "Sandy, I am sorry, but I am going to have to let you go; this is just not working out." Sandy had a stunned look on her face. "I tried to help you and give you enough time to change, but you didn't, and I'm sorry for that. You need to leave now; you have to see Anne so you can give her your badge and sign some paperwork. You're smart, and you're a good worker, so I know you'll find another job soon."

Sandy suddenly burst up from her chair and stood in front of Maria's face, screaming, "Why am I being fired?" There was a panicked look in Sandy's eyes. "You can't do this to me; I'm the best worker here!"

"You know, Sandy, it's hard for me to believe that you're asking me why you're being fired. Why do you think?" Maria asked. "I spoke to you so many times about your pot smoking in the office, and you denied it again and again."

"How dare you try and fire me! You're not going to get away with this, you know. I was here before you came."

"This office is about upholding the law, and that's important." Maria tried to be as professional as she could, but she could feel her insides shaking and wanted this all to be over. "Again, I'm very sorry it came to this, but I didn't fire you, you fired yourself."

"Don't give me that I'm sorry bit. You've been after me since you first came here. This is not over, not at all. You will be sorry you did this, I'll make sure of it."

"Are you threatening me?" Maria asked, trying to keep her voice calm. But she was disgusted by Sandy's aggressiveness and lack of any self-awareness. "Do I have to call security, or would you prefer to go quietly? I'm sure you're upset, that's understandable. But don't threaten me again," Maria said.

Sandy stared at Maria, squinting her eyes until they were almost closed. "I'm going now, but believe me you're going to regret this. It's not over between you and me." Sandy grabbed her things and stormed out of the office.

It wasn't long before Maria hired a replacement for Sandy, a sweet young girl who didn't smell of pot in the morning. But she lacked Sandy's spark of creativity and energy. Maria and Sandy had worked well together, revising procedures to improve the efficiency of the office. Sandy's willingness to adapt to changes, her enthusiasm, and her drive made Maria a more creative thinker. There were times when Maria questioned her decision to expose Sandy and fire her; she missed her.

"Can I help you find a book?" asked the clerk.

Maria was startled. Her mind jolted back to the bookstore, she just stared at him.

"Is there something in particular you're looking for?" he asked again.

"No, no thank you, I'm just looking around." She wanted this sales clerk just to go away and leave her alone. He could ruin everything.

Maria kept her eye on the door. She could feel the heat of her flushed face when she saw him enter the bookstore.

She waited until he walked to the back of the store. She had to move quickly, rushing out of her hiding place, bumping into a woman as she passed. She pushed open the exit doors, looking back several times to see if he was following. The hot summer air hit her face as she ran to her car. Her hands shook when she tried to put the key in the door. The keys slipped to the ground. She grabbed them off the pavement, turned back again to look out for him, then got in the car. She pushed down the door locks and started the car. She was shaking as she grabbed the sunshade and threw it in the back seat. Being in the locked car still didn't make her feel safe; she had to get out of there. As she sped out of the parking lot, passing the glass exit doors, she saw him. He was leaning against the wall smoking a cigarette. Had she just imagined he was following her?

Maria thought about telling someone at work about the incident, but she never did. It had been more than a year since the leather-vested man followed her in the mall. In the meantime, she had moved on to the felony department, as Rickie had promised. Gloria arranged a cake for her on the day of her move, but Maria knew there would be no tears from anyone there. She now had a real office with a window that overlooked the mountains.

It was a Monday morning. Maria began opening up the many case files piled on her desk. She started with a domestic violence case. These were among the most difficult cases to work. When she began reading the police report, she recognized the victim as her Sandy. There were several photos of her, one of her battered and bruised body with only her bra and panties on, another of her face showing both eyes black and blue, one eye practically swollen shut. She remembered Sandy's packed on face makeup, with the bruises showing through, and those long sleeve shirts she wore. The police report stated that a neighbor had called 911 after he heard a woman screaming. When the police arrived, they saw a man, Sandy's husband, standing over her body kicking her before they stopped him and made the arrest. Sandy was taken to the hospital; child protection services took the children. There was an arrest photo of the husband, and a written description that read, "scar over right eye." Maria recognized his face from the family photo on Sandy's desk. It started to make sense to her now. He was the man that followed her in the mall. What was he going to do to her if she hadn't gotten away? Did Sandy set this up? Or was he just angry that Maria fired her? After Sandy was fired did he beat her? Maria couldn't look at the photos any longer. She closed the file; her head was pounding.

Maria made sure she was in the courtroom for the verdict in this case. From her seat in the back, she could see Sandy seated in the front row, behind her husband, who was sitting next to his lawyer. When the guilty verdict was read, she saw Sandy bury her head in her hands and cry. When the husband turned around to look at Sandy, he saw Maria. Maria stared at him; he stared back, and then cocked his head up as though to say, "You're lucky you got away."

Maria left her seat and stood outside of the courtroom waiting for Sandy to come out. When Sandy opened the doors, Maria hardly recognized her; she was no longer hiding under heavy makeup. Her eyes were red and swollen; her bruises were a healing yellow and brown.

Maria approached her. "Sandy … I'm so sorry this happened to you. I wish I could have done more to help you."

"He has been beating me for years. The marijuana was to get me through to the next day." Sandy's face grew softer and sadder. "I guess in some way I hoped this would happen. No one can help me now; I'll probably lose my children." Sandy hurried away.

As Maria prepared to exit the plane, she kept thinking about the last time she saw Sandy. She was glad to be back in New York. She dragged her suitcase, stopped for a second and took a deep breath, inhaling the damp metal smell of New York City. The same smell she remembered each time she got off the train after it screeched into Grand Central Station. The smells and sounds of suburban New York were different; there was the scent of freshly cut grass, the sounds of chirping crickets at night, and the flickering glow of the fireflies. She found comfort in all these smells and sounds; it was home, even though she didn't live there anymore. It had been three years since she moved to Arizona for a new job. She thought, maybe the cold New York winters and the hot sticky summers weren't so bad after all.

Acknowledgments

I want to thank my husband, Eric, for reading and rereading my stories and for his willingness to be my actor when needed. Thank you to my son, Daniel, for his encouragement. Special thanks to my brother, Angelo, (aka creative genius) for all his help, especially with my titles. I am forever grateful to all my readers—Judy, Mary, Sharon, Lynn, Gloria, Sandy, Marilyn, Jackie, Yolanda, Ginger, Lisa and Kimberly—who gave me great comments, encouragement, and suggestions. I want to thank Mike Foley, editor and creator of The Writer's Edge, for his encouraging comments about my stories and for his inspirational monthly column. I am especially thankful to Ginger Benlifer for her insightful and thoughtful comments on my stories and characters. This book would not have happened without my amazingly talented editor and friend, Lauren O'Neill. She corrected my many mistakes and gave me the courage to stretch as a writer. Her creative suggestions polished the stories and made them so much better.

About the Author

Diana M. Grillo grew up in a struggling, Italian immigrant family while living in a wealthy suburb in Westchester County, New York. The neighborhood's substantial wealth and social status starkly contrasted with her family's, making Diana feel as though she never quite belonged. She became a mother at a very young age and worked her way through college while raising a son and daughter.

After graduating with a B.S. from Mercy College, Diana worked as a paralegal and social worker. Now retired, Diana currently lives in Cave Creek, Arizona with her husband where she has taken up writing short stories.

The sharp socio-economic contrasts of her youth and her tenacious journey into adulthood have inspired much of her work. Clearly, her realistic grasp on the struggles of the family is worth celebrating. Diana is a member of the Arizona Authors' Association. Her short story *Mr. Anderson* is featured in a Vinculinc Anthology, *Boundless, Stories By Authors Destined To Soar*. Diana's radio interview can be found on speakuptalkradio.com under the author series. Her website is shortstoriesbydiana.com

Made in the USA
Middletown, DE
04 May 2018